Quick Tips
for Better
Business Writing

Other Books by Gary Blake

THE STATUS BOOK

With Robert W. Bly:

TECHNICAL WRITING: STRUCTURE, STANDARDS, AND STYLE

DREAM JOBS: A GUIDE TO TOMORROW'S TOP CAREERS

HOW TO PROMOTE YOUR OWN BUSINESS

CREATIVE CAREERS: REAL JOBS IN GLAMOUR FIELDS

OUT ON YOUR OWN: FROM CORPORATE TO SELF-EMPLOYMENT

THE ELEMENTS OF BUSINESS WRITING

THE ELEMENTS OF TECHNICAL WRITING

Quick Tips for Better Business Writing

GARY BLAKE

McGraw-Hill, Inc.

New York   San Francisco   Washington, D.C.   Auckland   Bogotá
Caracas   Lisbon   London   Madrid   Mexico City   Milan
Montreal   New Delhi   San Juan   Singapore
Sydney   Tokyo   Toronto

Library of Congress Cataloging-in-Publication Data

Blake, Gary.
    Quick tips for better business writing / Gary Blake.
        p.   cm.
    Includes index.
    ISBN 0-07-005691-9 (pbk.)
    1. Business writing.   I. Title.
    HF5718.3.B535   1995
    808'.06665—dc20   95-3942
                                                          CIP

    5 6 7 8 9 0   DOC/DOC   9 0 0 9 8 7 6

ISBN 0-07-005691-9

*The sponsoring editor for this book was Betsy Brown, the editing
supervisor was Jane Palmieri, the designer was Fred Bernardi, and the
production supervisor was Donald Schmidt. It was set in Palatino by
Terry Leaden of McGraw-Hill's Professional Publishing Group
composition unit.*

Printed and bound by R. R. Donnelley & Sons Company.

McGraw-Hill books are available at special quantity discounts to
use as premiums and sales promotions, or for use in corporate
training programs. For more information, please write to the
Director of Special Sales, McGraw-Hill, Inc., 11 West 19th Street,
New York, NY 10011. Or contact your local bookstore.

To
Billy Blake
and
Carole Blake

Contents

Introduction

If you're looking for a safe topic of conversation for your next cocktail party, you need look no further than the decline of writing skills among recent college graduates.
Everyone will nod in agreement.

"No one knows how to punctuate a sentence anymore."

"The memos I see in my office make me chuckle."

"I see proposals that make no logical sense."

"My engineers don't know how to get to the point."

"No one knows how to write a paragraph; people just write bullets all the time!"

Many managers throughout the country look at the lack of writing skills as if it were bad weather: they complain about it but can't do anything about it.
Fortunately, that's changing.
Corporations are investing heavily in helping employees hone their writing skills. Top managers are complaining less about having to take on this training burden and concentrating instead on the bottom-line benefits of having employees who write clearly and concisely.
As someone who travels throughout the United States presenting on-site and public seminars in business writing, technical writing, proposal writing, and writing for systems professionals, I see the devastation that poor writing can have on an organization.

- People who receive little or no feedback on their writing soon stop trying to write well.

- People who are shaky about their writing skills are reluctant to put their good ideas in written form.

- Salespeople who are "good on their feet" lose sales because their prospects want them to put their ideas in writing.

- Systems analysts have trouble communicating with laypeople, and the result is time-wasting extra communications in which the analyst is asked to "explain what was meant" in the original memo.

- Lawyers, insurance professionals, and bankers use a Dickensian prose replete with *enclosed please find, under separate cover, herein,* and *pursuant to our conversation.*

Yes, there are big writing problems in the business world—and many books on the library shelves that address these problems. *Quick Tips for Better Business Writing* takes a slightly different approach than other books on the subject:

- *Quick Tips* applies itself to *more than two dozen of the most common business documents,* allowing readers to focus on the practical issues involved in writing a particular communication. In this book, the reader can access information about an encyclopedic range of business documents, not just letters, memos, and reports. The reader can focus on quality manuals, press releases, procedures, thank-you letters, and many other documents that receive only cursory mention in most writing books.

- *Quick Tips,* in addition to giving the reader a breadth of topics in the world of business communications, then offers *short, easy-to-grasp tips focused on each document.* So, for a person trying to write a press release, the tips in the press release section relate solely to the organization, wording, and editing of press releases.

- *Quick Tips* offers on-the-spot mentoring, helping business writers focus on the task at hand and gain a quick knowledge of the format and general boundaries of that particular business document. *Quick Tips* offers advice on organization, wording, and phrasing and provides the kind of consistent feedback and direction that is rarely present when an important document is about to be written and circulated. *Quick Tips* is your personal writing coach, providing fast help with the documents that you and your colleagues write at work.

The *Quick Tips* format leans heavily on numbered and bulleted bursts of advice. This doesn't mean that bullets are preferable to prose or a substitute for the type of involved discussion that paragraphs were invented to communicate. It is simply a format that was chosen for— and aids in—instant accessibility, in the same way that a résumé leans heavily on bullet points and underlining to get its message across in a matter of seconds.

As you use this book, you may think of many other tips on organizing, wording, and editing particular documents. I hope you'll share these thoughts with me. I'll make sure that your tips, fully credited, are considered for inclusion in future editions of *Quick Tips*.

You may write to me at:

The Communication Workshop
130 Shore Road, Dept. QT
Port Washington, NY 11050

Gary Blake

Acknowledgments

This book could not have been written without the help of many people who aided in the creation, phrasing, and editing of these tips.

Eve Blake, my wife and fellow language-lover, was responsible for formulating a great number of these tips, while collaborating with me on the writing of reports for *The Writer's Catalog*. Her clear-sighted, practical view of writing and editing is an ongoing inspiration to me as both a writer and teacher.

A lot of credit goes to the participants in my writing seminars, people from all over the United States who have shared with me their anxieties about the act of writing in a business environment and their fear of looking foolish on paper.

Thanks also to a number of human resource managers, training managers, and executives who have shown ongoing commitment to writing skills by offering communications seminars year after year. These include Don Begosh, Kay Wise, Eileen Ward, Bill Stewart, Dionne Ausby, David Lees, Don Fronzaglia, Carol S. Campbell, John Woody, Gary Allie, William Stewart, Al Halfacre, and Camille Cafferty.

A great big thank you to close associates and friends who have contributed to making these tips sharper, more helpful, and clearer. These people include Steve Meye rs, Millie Barnes, Deanne Junior, Bob Bly, and Richard Nelson.

Finally, thanks to Bonita K. Nelson, friend and agent, for her patience and fortitude and to Betsy Brown, my editor, who shaped the idea of "quick tips" and championed this book's cause at McGraw-Hill.

Gary Blake

THE 10 COMMANDMENTS OF BUSINESS WRITING

1. Prefer active language to passive language.

2. Prefer simple language to the elegant or complex.

3. Delete words, sentences, and phrases that do not add to your meaning.

4. Avoid sexist terms as well as politically incorrect stereotypes.

5. Use specific and concrete terms instead of vague generalities.

6. Avoid needlessly technical language.

7. Break the writing into short sections.

8. Keep ideas in writing parallel.

9. Use an informal rather than a formal style.

10. Write to express, not to impress.

PART 1
Letters

1

Sales Letters

Whole books have been written on writing effective sales letters, so I won't try to write another one here. I'll simply abstract five quick tips that provide an instant checklist of important issues to think about when organizing and phrasing letters meant to solicit new business.

✔ *1-1. Don't boast.*

The best selling is a straightforward discussion of the prospect's needs and how your products or services can meet those needs. Just present the facts. There should be little need to editorialize on the facts.

✔ *1-2. Keep persuasion moving.*

Using the persuasive sequence—gain attention, show a need, satisfy the need, show benefits, call for action—your letter can proceed briskly. Don't slow down the pace of your persuasion by getting into extraneous details or irrelevancies. Think of persuasion as a moving belt. Your job is to keep it moving until you call for the prospect to take a step toward the purchase.

✔ **1-3.** *Make each letter personal.*

Knock out all those tired phrases that scream "form letter" to the reader. Instead of *enclosed please find* use *I've enclosed.* The word *I,* by the way, is valuable in keeping your writing personal. Other phrases to avoid: *under separate cover, very truly yours, pursuant to your request,* and *as per our discussion.*

Since people are fond of official recognition, always include the person's name—spelled correctly—as well as his or her title. And if you know the person, or had a friendly meeting with the person, include some personal details that will warm up your message.

✔ **1-4.** *Anticipate the prospect's questions.*

Place yourself in the prospect's shoes. What questions would you have about your own products? Price? Advantages over other products? Try to understand and appreciate anything that might give your prospect reason to hesitate about buying and then deal with those reasons in your letter. Also, remember that your prospect may not understand some of the technical information you need to convey, so beware of too much jargon. Explain technical terms your reader might not know.

✔ **1-5.** *Don't let the prospect slip away.*

Entrepreneurs would starve if they wrote the same kind of vague closings to letters that are common inside big organizations. Tell the prospect what will happen next. Don't just end with a "see you around" kind of wishy-washiness.

2

Cover Letters

Recently, a woman applying for a secretarial position at my company sent me a résumé and a cover letter. Unlike so many cover letters I've seen, her letter spoke directly to my needs instead of simply regurgitating her résumé. Here's how her cover letter read:

> Dear Mr. Blake:
>
> Do you ever wish that when you're out training, someone could be back at your office typing sales letters and keeping things organized?
>
> That's where I can help.
>
> If I come to work for The Communication Workshop, I'll help you send out 50 sales letters a day and make sure that all of the calls that come in get proper attention. I could help you take care of all the clerical details so that you could concentrate on presenting the writing course itself.
>
> So, I'll give you a call next week to discuss ways in which I can help you increase your business and help you find better ways to look after the many details involved in presenting your seminars.
>
> Sincerely,

Now, *that's* a cover letter. The applicant had obviously

done her homework. She knew enough about my small consulting firm to pitch her letter directly at one of my chief needs—to clone myself in order to handle more business.

To see why this letter works so well, let's first analyze its organization:

> *Gain attention:* The opening sentence is a rhetorical question that catches the reader's attention; it directly relates to a problem the owner of a small consulting firm would have.

> *Show a need:* In that same opening sentence, the writer crystallizes my need for someone who can organize my office while I'm out conducting seminars.

> *Satisfy the need:* It's only after suggesting a need that it makes sense for the writer to step forward to suggest that there is a solution. Actually, *she* is the solution: "That's where I can help."

> *Visualize results:* Now that we know the solution, the writer must demonstrate just how she plans to be of help. She does this by walking me into the future, a happy future in which she is already valuable to me and to my company. She is forcing me to visualize the results of her "solution" to my need—hiring her. While she details the type of duties she can perform to help me improve my business, she never mentions the words *hire* or *job.*

> *Call for action:* After making me visualize many of the ways she'll be of value, she has me right where she wants me. She is now ready to close the letter. Most job seekers would have made several critical errors at this point. They might have given their phone number and asked me to call them to discuss coming in for an interview. She doesn't. She says that she'll call me. In addition, although many job seekers would write to set up an interview about "a job," this writer continues to focus on

the reader's need by saying that the discussion will be about ways in which she can help the reader improve his business.

Here are some cover-letter-writing tips:

✔ **2-1.** *Avoid the trap of regurgitating your résumé.*

Most people simply enumerate points made on the résumé, which makes either document unnecessary. The trick in writing an effective cover letter is to select highlights that you think are significant for your reader and that you'd like the reader to focus on.

✔ **2-2.** *Avoid boastful statements.*

In an attempt to dramatize certain skills, many people slip inadvertently into opinionated statements about themselves. Here's a typical example: "I am a very well-rounded and active individual with a great deal of discipline." Says you. Don't tell the reader what you can do: Show the reader by using facts about yourself, not opinions.

✔ **2-3.** *Avoid trite language and jargon.*

Potential employers, like other readers, will be turned off by words and expressions that sound dull and unoriginal. Such phrases include:

Attached herewith is my résumé

Please find enclosed my résumé

As per your ad…

Thanking you in advance

I am writing to inquire about career opportunities…

Awaiting the pleasure of a favorable response

If you have any questions, please do not hesitate to call.

✔ **2-4.** *Find the name of the person who'll hire you and address your cover letter to that person.*

That means you'll have to do your homework before sending out cover letters that are unrequested by a company. The work will pay off for two reasons: (1) it shows initiative, and (2) letters addressed to individuals get faster attention.

If you're responding to a blind advertisement, which gives a box number without the name of a person or a company, you obviously cannot address someone directly. But you can still customize the cover letter. Review the ad to see what the advertiser emphasizes. Look for phrases such as *applicant must have* or *necessary qualifications include* as keys for vital characteristics to emphasize about yourself.

If the ad contains a company name, call and ask for the name of the person who's hiring. Be sure to get the correct spelling of the name and title.

✔ **2-5.** *Make sure that your "gain attention" opening does just that.*

In response to a blind ad, for example, someone responding to a particularly enticing ad wrote: "I'm sure that the stack of résumés on your desk must be eye level by now. Here's why this one should be on top." This opening used the power of empathy and humor to get response. Avoid cliché openings such as "This is in response to your ad in today's..." or "Your advertisement in today's *Times* caught my eye."

You may use quotations, startling statements, rhetorical statements, provocative questions—anything that will interest the reader and is pertinent to the particular job you're seeking.

✔ **2-6.** *Whenever possible, avoid asking readers to call you—say you'll call them.*

By doing this, you "program" the recipient to expect your call. You are taking the initiative, separating yourself from the crowd of people who hope that the employer will pick up the phone to call.

3

Electronic Mail (E-Mail)

In the past five years, many people in the technical community have become used to transmitting information within their organizations by E-mail (electronic mail), an informal way of sending messages between computer terminals. E-mail has cut photocopying drastically at many companies. It has also cut interoffice mail and time on the telephone by up to 90 percent.

People like to send E-mail because they find it easier to use than other print media and better for eliciting follow-up. People like to receive E-mail because they can reread it, save it, and forward messages, an advantage over telephone and face-to-face conversations.

But E-mail has turned out to be a mixed blessing. Its very speed and informality have led to misunderstandings and mis-distributions that might have never happened if the messages were sent in a slower and unautomated mode.

E-mail is now widely available, capable of reaching destinations worldwide often for less cost than a telephone call or even postage. Its origins in the research and academic communities, combined with its rapid rise in popularity, have created technical standards for how computers are to address and deliver E-mail but have left standards for content and style up to each sender. Following are a few guidelines for good E-mail use:

✔ **3-1.** *Use E-mail instead of memos, when possible.*

Instead of cluttering up people's desks with memos (and wasting paper), use E-mail. It's great to use E-mail for communicating with one person or with 100 people. But to make E-mail effective, check messages frequently, and don't let them pile up.

✔ **3-2.** *Compose the subject line carefully.*

Don't make the subject line too general, e.g., Subject: Writing seminar. Instead, narrow it to encapsulate your precise message, e.g., Subject: Suggested candidates for January writing seminar. A subject line should do more than suggest the general topic; it should summarize the point of the message. Ask yourself: What do you want the reader to know, do, or believe as a result of the message? If you want a go ahead to hire a temp, your memo's subject isn't just "Hiring a temp," it's "Request to hire a temp for next week."

✔ **3-3.** *Keep it short.*

Short messages are appropriate for E-mail. Lengthy documents sent unsolicited to numerous recipients are inappropriate. Just because you can push a button and share your missive with the multitudes, don't give in to the temptation to share every bright idea you have with worldwide colleagues. Also, it's better to send a message announcing the availability of the document than the document itself.

Although E-mail started out as a handy way to send short messages, some people piggyback new messages on top of the original messages, often causing confusion. Once you start piggybacking messages, you stand a chance of fouling up everyone else's message as well as your own. It's better to just write a separate message.

Keep each message to one topic. This way you increase the chances your readers will read and understand what you write.

✔ **3-4.** *Be consistent.*

Since E-mail is so informal, there is a tendency to write in short, staccato sentences and phrases; to keep the message in all capital letters; and generally to ignore the rules of punctuation and spacing. Appearance still counts. Treat your E-mail the same as any other professional communication.

Send messages in both upper- and lowercase letters. All uppercase letters make your message hard to read; all lowercase messages are hard to read and unprofessional looking.

✔ **3-5.** *Restrain the urge to "return fire."*

The immediacy of E-mail may make the recipient feel compelled to compose an immediate response. Don't be hasty, especially if you are responding to an E-mail message that has made you angry or defensive.

Be diplomatic. E-mail's convenient reach can be a drawback, because it makes it easier to insult or alienate recipients. Remember that E-mail is irrevocable and permanent. Don't write in anger, and stay away from profanity. Cool down before hitting your "send" button.

✔ **3-6.** *Be sure to refer to the original message.*

For example, if you receive a meeting notice, mention it in your reply: "I will attend the meeting scheduled for" or "Re: Your E-mail message of 9/10/XX, 9:08 a.m.," instead of, "I will attend" or "Yes, I'll be there."

On some E-mail systems, the original "Re" line automatically remains the same when you are responding to a message.

✔ **3-7.** *Paraphrase when necessary.*

Since E-mail has a feature that allows a recipient of a message to add some comments and forward it, a short message can become a lengthy chain of comments. Rather than perpetuate the chain of messages, paraphrase the comments and original message. A sample paraphrase: "I received a meeting notice for August 12, 19XX, at 9 a.m., but John, Joe, and Mary all said they can't attend, so please reschedule it."

This paraphrase is more concise than three separate messages saying: (1) I received a meeting notice for August 12, 19XX, at 9 a.m., (2) I received word that John, Joe, and Mary will not be able to attend that August 12th meeting, and (3) Will you please reschedule the meeting to a time when we can all attend?

✔ **3-8.** *Guard confidential information.*

It's too easy for such information to accidentally get into the wrong hands. Realize that E-mail can be misaddressed as well as forwarded. As a general guideline, don't send anything via E-mail that you don't want to see on the front page of your company newsletter or local newspaper.

4

Fund-Raising Letters

How do you get strangers to contribute to your cause? Traditionally, they are wooed in many ways, with direct-mail solicitation being only one of those ways. Still, according to a Gallup survey, 30 percent of the people who gave to a charity for the first time did so because they received a letter asking them to give.

Universities, hospitals, charities, civic organizations, and political parties use a variety of other techniques, including door-to-door canvassing, parties, telephone solicitation, personal requests, and posters. Direct mail, however, is still an effective way of telling your organization's story to a very large audience.

Millions of words have been written about the various elements of how to write fund-raising letters—how long? How short? How personal? Many, many variables will determine the success of a letter—the quality and amount of the writing are only two of the factors. Other intrinsic factors include your choice of an outside envelope, use of photos, inclusion of a premium, reply card, and return envelope. Extrinsic factors that will influence your response include the aptness and quality of your mailing list, the timing of your mailing, and the frequency of your mailing.

Let's not regurgitate information about the need for testing everything or the fact that 92 percent of your mail will never even be opened or that direct mail works best in a sustained effort over a number of years—you know all that. The tips will concern the intrinsic message—the words, the look, the appeal—of your direct mail.

✔ **4-1.** *Use emotion, controversy, and surprise to catch your readers' attention.*

Nothing rivets a reader like an attention-getting device centered on controversy and emotion. Here are a few wonderful samples of clever attention-getting devices:

For the American Israel Public Affairs Committee:

The outside envelope asks: "Whose dream shall survive?"

Pictured is Yasir Arafat, saying, "We shall not rest...until we destroy Israel."

Next to his picture is one of Golda Meir, saying, "Peace is the dream."

Here's how a pitch letter from a major opera company begins:

Dear Friend of the Opera:

Do you remember the first time you went to the opera? Quite a thrill, wasn't it?

This rhetorical question opening pulls the reader into the message by focusing on the thrill of a theatrical experience.

One film legend's appeal letter for Planned Parenthood is a model for striking a note of instant controversy:

Dear Friend,

Normally, I don't get involved in public controversy. But reproductive freedom is a basic, *personal* issue, and one that I feel very strongly about for personal reasons....

Here's how a letter of appeal from a nature association stirs the emotions and begins to outline a controversy:

Dear Investor:

The bug-eyed bird on our envelope who's ogling you with such distemper has a point. He's a native American sandhill crane and you may be sitting on one of his nesting sites....

Or, from the Sea Turtle Rescue Fund:

Dear Friend:

For just $15.67 you can "adopt" a nest of green turtle eggs in Mexico and take part in a unique project designed to help rescue these wonderful creatures from extinction.

✔ **4-2.** *Add a personal touch.*

If you're writing to share a highly personal story about your own life, and if that story is directly related to the appeal you are making, you're almost certain to win over your reader.

Look at the opening to the appeal letter from a leading actress on behalf of the Girl Scout Council of Greater New York:

Dear Friend,

I am writing to you not as an actress—but as the mother of a Girl Scout and as a Girl Scout Leader. *I know how valuable the Girl Scout experience is because I know how much happiness and personal fulfillment it brought me and my daughter Mary before she died of polio when she was just 19....*

Here are some other ways to add a personal touch to your fund-raising pitches:

1. Don't typeset your letter. Reproduce it from perfectly typewritten copy. Typeset letters, by definition, aren't personal.

2. Don't omit the salutation ("Dear Friend"), and do try to include a date line if possible. They are part of the real letter look.

3. Pretend you are writing to one person. Indeed you are.

4. Don't use big words or jargon.

Also, be aware of using your *P.S.* wisely, because it will be read. Too many postscripts just take up space.

✔ **4-3.** *Be aware of impressions.*

If you get too fancy, your prospective donor may think that you're spending money frivolously, so avoid stationery that's too fancy or expensive. You don't want a mailing piece that calls attention to itself as being too extravagant, so stay away from 4-color printing—especially if you're asking for donations to a charity.

One impression that you do want to give is that of being appreciative for past donations. Every donation must be acknowledged—just as you would send thanks for any gift, but also because people who feel appreciated are likely to give even more generously the next time. For large gifts, a handwritten note is best.

Your thank-you letter should acknowledge the gift, give some interesting news about your charity's recent activities, and "plant the seed" that future gifts will be welcome.

Here's how a New York City shelter for addicted babies recently acknowledged a small donation:

Dear Friends,

Just a short note to let you know we received your recent gift of $25. Lord knows, we sure need your help this month. Thank you for being so generous!

Since the last time I wrote to you, we've had a few

additions to Hale House. Little Amanda is the most recent, and the smallest. Bless her heart, she is so tiny, you'd think she was only 3 months old, but her first birthday was last month.

We'll never know the horrors we rescued these babies from just by being here. So many were malnourished and even physically abused by their parents. Drugs do terrible things to people.

Thank you for being so faithful in helping us help these babies. Your gifts not only help provide the money to buy food, clothes, toys, and medicine for our babies, it also encourages me. It is so nice to know you are standing with us.

Please write to us again soon.

Warm regards,

P.S. The needs never stop at our facility, and summer brings a new set of expenses. I hope you will help us again when you can.

This is a masterful tickler letter. It joins hands with the reader and bathes the reader in a glow of good feeling. The letter closes gently: "Please write to us again soon." It would be too blatant to turn this letter of thanks into a brand new pitch. Yet, the writer is aware that this is, like all communications from Hale House, a pitch for more money because the need for money is continuous. So, the writer uses a P.S., always an attention getter, to leave no doubt in the reader's mind that a new donation would be appreciated.

✔ **4-4.** *Follow a persuasive sequence.*

There are variations on a basic sequence that many successful fund-raising letters use. Here's one version of the sequence:

1. Create interest
2. State the problem

3. Arouse emotion

4. Offer hope

5. Offer participation

6. Induce response (ask for the gift)

7. Offer thanks

Here's "the perfect fund-raising letter." The letter, interestingly, is written from a boy to his aunt. The request for money is handled as smoothly and professionally as any direct-mail pitch ever written:

Dear Aunt Bessie:

It hasn't been any fun being sick in bed for two weeks, but the books you sent helped pass the time. Thank you for being such a sweet, thoughtful aunt.

You know how much I'd looked forward to going to camp this summer—but the doc said "no way"; it's another three to five weeks in bed and then weeks of rehabilitation until I'm my old self.

Oh well, I was torn trying to decide whether to be a pro football player or a best-selling writer. I guess we both know which it will be (bet you're happy, huh, Aunt Bess?).

Speaking of writing, I saw an ad in the classifieds for a used portable electric typewriter. I won't beat around the bush. It costs $145. But I could use the allowance I haven't been spending so far this summer, which would amount to almost $45 by next month.

What do you say, Aunt Bess? For a $100 investment in your favorite nephew, you might get to read a brilliant crime novel by Labor Day! Not only would it help me from going bonkers, it would make you happy too.

Because I've always been able to count on you before in times of *real* need (and Aunt Bess, you taught me a lot about not asking for silly things), I called the phone number in the ad, and the man said he'd hold it for three days. So if you're going to say yes, please do it soon—it's an emergency! His name is Mr. Brel, and his phone number is 213-2132.

And again, if you can't afford the whole typewriter, I'll understand. But would you be able to send $50? I can add my $30 and Mr. Brel will take installments, and Mom says she can also give $50 next month.

You see, I'm really determined to write that book—*with your help.*

I love you, and thanks.

Your Nephew,

Kevin

P.S. Here is a photo of me in the hospital with my leg in traction. Cute, huh?

✔ **4-5.** *Use simple language.*

Multisyllable words, lengthy sentences, and oblique references are the enemies of clear fund-raising style. You must write the way you speak, avoiding too much colloquialism or slang but also avoiding lawyerlike phrases such as *enclosed please find, under separate cover,* or *in lieu of.*

Think of Nancy Reagan's anti-drug slogan: "Just say NO!" You can't get any simpler than that.

The following letter is a fine example of how simple language can make a potent point:

Dear Mr. Caswell:

There are few causes that are so close to my heart that they could induce me to write you a letter like this; but on this occasion I feel I must appeal to you.

My home town of Racine is one of those expanding communities that has outgrown its recreational facilities. We are, therefore, building an addition to our Community Center that will be almost entirely for the use of children. To keep them off the streets, we are planning classrooms, game rooms, hobby rooms, a gymnasium, and other facilities for supervised activities.

In order to provide the necessary funds, we are publishing a journal in connection with a dinner-dance to be held on March 4th. This letter is to ask you to buy advertising space in this journal.

It is not easy for me to write to you in this way, but I am sure you understand the importance of the cause.

Please say yes!

With sincere thanks,

P.S. Of course, the advertisement is a deductible item on next year's income tax.

This letter, which reads like conversation, has very few multisyllable words and is about as direct as one can get. It could be understood by a 10-year-old child.

Again, don't use a big word when a small one will do: *gift* instead of *donation, use* instead of *utilize,* and *best* instead of *optimum.*

5

Collection Letters

When payment of your invoice is overdue, what do you do? If you start phoning the debtor, you may become frustrated and say things that may lose your customer as well as your money. It's easy to start threatening legal action, for example, but you're sure to lose what could be a good customer. The object is to get your money and to keep your customer.

Here are some quick tips on writing collection letters:

✔ **5-1.** *Be prepared to write several letters to collect money owed to you.*

One letter may not be enough to remind, motivate, or threaten the person to pay up. It's best to start with a gentle reminder and escalate in severity and pressure. Each letter in the series should be written as if you expect it to be the last.

✔ **5-2.** *Know that even the best letters may fail.*

Alas, there's no surefire formula for such letters nor any exact way of determining each one's timing. The real art of controlling credit is to assess your risk so you are not dependent on letters to get payment out of a bad payer. Letters won't force a customer to pay, especially if the debtor has no money or no intention of paying.

✔ **5-3.** *Make your letters progressively more confrontational.*

As your letters keep getting ignored, you have an obligation to turn up the heat. Your appeals will go from nice to nasty. Here is a typical series of appeals:

☐ Statement that account is past due.

☐ Statement that account was overlooked.

☐ May we ask if there is something wrong?

☐ Appeal to fair play.

☐ Appeal for maintenance of good credit.

☐ Threat of posting with credit agencies.

☐ Threat of legal action.

☐ Resort to legal action.

☐ Lawyer's letter threatening suit.

☐ Serving of summons.

✔ **5-4.** *In your first letter, assume the customer wants to pay and just needs a little reminding.*

No need to editorialize or show anger. I once saw a letter that began "It is inconceivable that you didn't realize that your payment was due on June 15th." I would simply have written: "Your payment was due on June 15th. It is now September 15th, and we have not received it...." The facts themselves can be more damning—or shaming—than any display of anger or disappointment contained in your venting. Stick to the facts.

✔ **5-5.** *Before writing a second reminder, let some time go by to give the debtor an opportunity to send the payment.*

After all, maybe the debtor has been ill, on vacation, or away on business. The second reminder might look something like this:

Dear _____

Re: Account No. _____ Invoice No. _____

May we remind you that this account is overdue for payment?

We remind you that our terms are 30 days, and we supply goods on the understanding of payment by the proper time.

Please send us a check by return mail.

✔ **5-6.** *If you still haven't received payment or heard from the debtor, you should "turn up the heat" a bit.*

Here's an example of how this letter might be written:

According to our records, $536.82 is outstanding on your account and is now considerably overdue for payment.

Since you have not responded to our previous reminder, I now have no option but to hold up the supply of any further orders until your account has been settled.

If you have any questions concerning your account, please call me at _____. If I don't hear from you by July 10, we will take further measures to recover our debt.

✔ **5-7.** *Be firm, consistent, and courteous. Some will respond to your persistence, knuckling under to your demand for payment.*

You can always tell your customer that you are closing the books on a particular accounting cycle and need payment. Another tactic is to appeal to the debtor's pride ("We know you don't want to ruin your fine credit rating by being placed on our delinquent list"). For some, this may appeal to the need to make a fresh start without penalty.

✔ **5-8.** *Eventually, you may have to produce more compelling arguments.*

...Like rubbing in the guilt ("...Credit is extended as a courtesy to our customers...") or mild threats ("We would not want to place you on our delinquent list") to greater threats ("We would not like to be forced to contact the people who oversee your credit rating...").

After you've tried everything, you'll be faced with a few final choices: (1) cut off—if you haven't already—the supply of goods to the customer, (2) contact a collection agency, or (3) take legal action. At this point, there's little sense in worrying about keeping the customer—you want your payment and are ready to go to court.

6

Thank-You Letters

Just as one of the great skills in writing a love song is to not use the phrase "I love you," one of the great arts of writing a thank-you letter is to find original or even unique ways of saying "thank you."

Two of the main types of thank-you letters you're likely to write are those in which you thank someone for something they've done for you and those in which you thank someone for giving you something.

As for the first of these, you want to show your appreciation without sounding overly humble; as for thanking people for gifts, you want to make the giver feel that the gift was more than just a lucky guess at what you wanted: it's the right gift because the right person made a clever decision based on your long-standing relationship—at least, that's the ideal!

Here are some tips on writing your own thank-you letters:

✔ **6-1.** *Find new and different ways to say "thank you."*

It's one thing to thank someone for sending you a box of Havana cigars by saying "Thank you for the wonderful cigars." It's another to say that you can't wait until you can put your feet up, lie back, and start to take your first puff.

✔ **6-2.** *Avoid the other clichés of thank-you letters.*

Don't thank people for their time. Yes, I know a lot of people do it, but I feel it takes away from the equality that should exist in a business relationship. When you write, "Thanks for taking five minutes from your busy schedule," you are being overly humble, putting the recipient on a pedestal, and making it seem as though the five minutes was a precious gift. It wasn't. There should be some mutuality. It's better to say "Thanks for meeting with me" or "I enjoyed meeting with you."

Also avoid such clichés as "How very kind of you," "Thanks for your most generous gift," and "I'm sure I will put your gift to good use."

✔ **6-3.** *As with the illustration about the gift of cigars, try to paint a picture of how you'll use the gift.*

So, instead of thanking the person for the nifty book, write something like, "As you know, I love reading about Zen and will await the moment when I can read *How to Meditate* without having the phone ringing, the doorbell buzzer buzzing, or my eight-year-old asking me to put the chicken nuggets in the microwave."

When you receive cash, you may feel awkward about acknowledging the gift in a note, but, again, think of how you'll use it and what it will mean in your life and communicate that feeling to the giver. One early retiree, who runs a booth at a flea market and received a check for $500 from a business owner wrote, "Your gift means a lot to me. In winter, it will be the difference between taking a taxi or waiting for the bus; in summer, it will mean being able to cover the flea markets of Long Island without having to count pennies. In short, your gift gives me a cushion. As the author Ben Hecht wrote, 'What is life without a sudden cushion?'"

✔ **6-4.** *Communicate how meaningful the gift is by referring to your relationship with the giver.*

The best thank-you letters communicate a sense not only of joy in the gift but of joy in the relationship with the gift's giver. It isn't that the giver gave you a book you had wanted to read, it's that the giver knew just the right book because she or he knows your taste and is sensitive to the range of books that are appropriate.

Someone who chooses the right clothing to give you isn't just lucky; he or she has taste and chose a color that is perfect. The emphasis in a thank-you letter should be balanced between appreciation of the gift itself and appreciation of the effort and thought that went into it.

✔ **6-5.** *Don't link a thank-you letter with a pitch for new business.*

It can be done, but it takes tremendous skill to do it. Most of the time, your reader will think that he or she was being thanked just so that you could begin to pitch for new business.

Get in the habit of writing thank-you letters that do nothing but say "thank you." That way, your message won't arouse undue suspicion. Later on, in a separate letter, you can open the door to new business.

If you are making a brief thank-you for kindnesses shown while you were in a person's place of business, you can, on occasion, link that with a thought such as "I intend to follow up with the training director at your sister company by calling him next week and mentioning that our seminar went quite well." You are not pitching for business so much as reminding your contact that you are about to make the new contact that was given to you. In this way, you are gently reminding the person who offered you the new contact's name to be ready in case she or he receives a call about you from this new contact.

7

Letters of Recommendation

At some point, you may be asked to write a letter of recommendation for a subordinate, colleague, or friend. Since this type of writing is sometimes looked at as a "chore," you may want to write a brief note and be done with it.

Don't. It's not fair to the person who is being recommended. By being superficial, you'll give the impression that the person under discussion is not really very interesting, much less extraordinary.

Here are a few tips on keeping your letters of recommendation sharp:

✔ *7-1. Show, don't tell.*

It's nice to say that "During the past 12 months that Tim has been with the company, he has continuously shown the willingness and commitment to perform all tasks assigned," but it's better to give some examples.

Was Tim able to pick up WordPerfect after only a few days? Did he volunteer for duty that was optional? Did he take the lead in forming a task force to look into a problem? Put down the specifics that will bolster your claims.

✔ **7-2.** *Show measurable, observable behavior.*

"Tim is an integral member of the Delaware team" doesn't give the reader anything to visualize or quantify. If you said that Tim supervises five people or has worked seven Saturdays in a row or hasn't missed a day in two years, you are telling the reader something measurable and quantifiable. Since there is often a lot of malarkey in letters of recommendation, yours should be specific and filled with facts that could be verified.

✔ **7-3.** *Show the fit between applicant and job.*

When you recommend someone for a promotion, you need to show that the person not only has done a great job in his or her present post but is capable of assuming the new responsibilities implied in a promotion.

Comment on the person's leadership skills: How does she or he manage people? Handle crises? Does the person keep his or her head in an emergency? Comment on the person's ability to manage time, to be productive. Point out precisely why a transition to a new job will be smooth. In short, get your reader to visualize the applicant as already productive in the new position.

PART 2

Reports and Memos

8

Memos

Although many aspects of memo writing have become conventional, many mistakes are still made in the organization, phrasing, and format of these common business documents. Here are ten quick tips to help you improve the format and content of your next memo:

✔ **8-1.** *Organize the list of names receiving your memo in alphabetical order.*

People worry about offending the secondary readers listed at the top of a memo or the people whose names appear in a "cc" list at the bottom of the memo (even though carbon copy has become an outdated concept, people still use "cc" as an abbreviation for "courtesy copy").

Although some companies require that these lists be organized according to rank, other companies are uncomfortable with this organizing principle. For example, how do you list several vice presidents of equal rank? You'd hate to offend someone by mistakenly writing his or her name below that of someone reporting to him or her.

To solve all such problems, it's best to take an "ensemble" approach to these listings. List the memo's secondary readers in alphabetical order, allowing people of different rank to appear in the democratic ordering. In the same way, in some theatrical and TV productions, cast members are listed alphabetically, without regard to their show business status.

✔ **8-2.** *Use* Re *and* Subject *lines appropriately.*

Re, Latin for *thing,* means "in the matter of" or "as regards." A *Re* line in a memo tells the reader that the memo's content is "in the matter of…" a particular topic— a meeting, a raise, a promotion, and so on.

A *Subject* line has a broader feel to it than a *Re* line. Some memos use both, e.g., "Subject: Fall promotion plan; Re: Responsibilities for each marketing group."

The *Subject* line is like the title of a book. It paints a broad picture of the topic. A *Re* line is similar to a subtitle, narrowing the scope of the broad title.

✔ **8-3.** *Sign your memo for an added personal touch.*

Some do, some don't. It's a subjective judgment. People who don't sign them usually explain that a signature is redundant because the memo already identifies the sender. Also, they associate a signature with a letter. Finally, some may feel that signing a memo may too closely identify the writer with topics or a group effort referred to in the memo. Some people prefer to initial the memo next to their name.

Signing your memo makes good sense for several reasons. We sign letters, even though we have our typed name in the letter as well, because signing adds a personal touch. Also, signing adds a sense of responsibility: You take responsibility for the memo's content and phrasing. For these reasons, we recommend signing memos.

✔ **8-4.** *Use the recipient's name within the memo for an additional personal touch.*

Some people start memos by using the name of the person to whom they are writing, e.g., "Bob, I just want to let you know that...." Some may feel that this is unnecessary or an affectation, but I believe that it's a way of "warming up" the tone of the communication. After all, salutations are not part of the form of a memo the way they are in letters; therefore, addressing your reader by name in the first sentence is one way of establishing personal connection.

We believe that people enjoy the sound of their own names. So, I see nothing wrong with using this as a way to start a memo in which you have a single reader with whom you are on a first-name basis.

✔ **8-5.** *Don't overdo jargon or buzz words, even if you're writing to someone who knows their meaning.*

When you are writing to a person who you're sure knows your field's jargon or buzz words, go ahead and use them. But when secondary readers are involved, think twice about throwing around jargon. Often, your memos are seen by many others besides those to whom they're addressed. Therefore, don't use jargon to "impress"; use simple words to "express."

✔ **8-6.** *Beware of lengthy paragraphs!*

There is no "correct" length for a paragraph, but you should try to keep opening paragraphs to fewer than 6 lines and subsequent paragraphs to within 12 lines.

Even though a paragraph may be defined as a cluster of like ideas, the reader's brain can only hold so much information at one time. Therefore, when you start writing paragraphs longer than 12 lines, ask yourself: "Can I divide this paragraph into two smaller paragraphs, each with its own idea or theme?"

✔ **8-7.** *Prefer the active to the passive voice.*

Active language is preferred because it is dynamic and authoritative. It shows people taking responsibility for their actions.

In fairness to the passive voice, sometimes it is more appropriate than the active voice: when the thing being done is more important than the doer of the action. "The shop opened at 9 a.m." is preferable to "John opened the shop at 9 a.m.," because the shop's opening is more important than who opened it.

Second, use passive language when you purposely want to soften a thought. Instead of writing "Please send me the check today," you might write "I'd appreciate receiving your check by Thursday."

✔ **8-8.** *Put enough background material in your memo so that a reader can understand the topic under discussion.*

It's always difficult to know just how much background information to put in a memo. After all, your primary reader may know the memo's background, but secondary readers may need to be oriented to the topic.

You can aid those secondary readers by including a brief recap of past events pertaining to the memo's topic. You usually need not spend several paragraphs or pages recapping the whole history of a project before diving into the current project issues. You can recap things in a line or two: "As you know, this is one of three methods we agreed to pursue for our new marketing effort; the other two we decided to shelve until 1996 because they are too time-consuming and require new workstations."

✔ **8-9.** *End your memo on your last thought.*

Don't succumb to the temptation of throwing in a gratuitous phrase like, "If you have any questions please call" (they will anyway) or "Thank you in advance for your cooperation." (Thanking in advance doesn't motivate the reader to do what you want; it's presumptuous.)

✔ **8-10.** *Use lots of white space.*

Keep margins wide (at least 1¼ inches on each side and on the top and bottom). Avoid overcapitalization. Use a readable typeface (serif) and size (at least 9-pt type). Skip two spaces between the date, *To* line, *From* line, *Re* line, and the body of the memo. Never use both sides of a piece of paper.

9

Meeting Minutes

Here are 10 tips on organizing and writing meeting minutes:

✔ **9-1.** *Put the list of attendees where the reader does not have to read it first.*

Although you must record who attended the meeting, you need not start with a list of attendees. Either put the list of attendees at the top right side of the page or else at the end of the minutes. By doing this, you allow the reader to immediately focus on the substance of the minutes.

✔ **9-2.** *Give an overview in the first paragraph.*

Many people merely list the day and time of the meeting and where it was held. But that's the kind of information that should be relegated to the Subject line.

Instead, give your readers a brief summary of the meeting as a whole, for example, "The IMS meeting was held to review the pending and completed items of the past month. Particular attention was given to the problems of system testing and year-end pricing, neither of which has been resolved."

✔ **9-3.** *Recognize that meetings usually involve information, discussion, and decisions.*

Not all meetings are well organized, but you have to be. If the meeting meanders from topic to topic, you have to impose an order on what you've recorded.

In most meetings, three things happen. Sometimes, people simply pass along information, and this information does not require any type of discussion or decision. Other topics require discussion, and your job is to summarize the key points that are raised. But the heart of most meetings is decision. After a reasonable amount of discussion, a decision is reached and that decision, as well as its ramifications for future meetings, should be highlighted in your minutes.

✔ **9-4.** *Cluster agenda items into sections.*

To make sure that your minutes do not read like a laundry list of random topics covered at the meeting, you need to cluster like items. For example, if 10 topics were discussed at a meeting, don't just number from 1 to 10. Instead, try to see similarities among topics. Perhaps five can be grouped under a section titled *Pending*, and the others may be grouped under *Completed*.

✔ **9-5.** *Organize a long list of pending or completed agenda items in order of importance.*

If you have only two or three items grouped under *Pending*, you may want to list the subjects in any particular order. But if your list is longer, there should be specific order to it (e.g., most important to least important). When this isn't possible, you may want to use a chronological arrangement, describing the agenda items that require immediate action first.

✔ **9-6.** *Use subheads.*

When you read this chapter, your eyes scan the pages and you readily see the main topics; then you read the details. That's because we've listed the items from 1 to 10, and we've highlighted and labeled the main points. You can—and should—do the same.

✔ **9-7.** *Keep ideas parallel.*

As in all writing, keep your ideas parallel. If you list four things that Mr. Heyward did at the meeting, write them this way:

Mr. Heyward:
- □ Mentioned...
- □ Reported...
- □ Explained...
- □ Requested...

✔ **9-8.** *Avoid excessive detail.*

It's your job to sort out important from unimportant details. By being selective, you avoid the "He said this, she said that" kind of writing. No one wants to know everything that was said. People want to know the key points of a discussion, the decisions that were reached, and the implications of each decision for the readers of the minutes. When responsibilities are delegated and deadlines are set, make sure that your minutes reflect who will be responsible for what by when.

✔ **9-9.** *Separate fact from opinion.*

While taking minutes, keep attuned to the difference between fact and opinion. Facts are objective and indisputable; opinions are personal views. Take this sentence: "The high percentage of unmatched records in the run could be due to the lack of editing and validation performed." Whose idea is this? Attribute opinions to their source (e.g., "Ms. Jones thought..." or "The group decided that...").

✔ **9-10.** *Mention the date of the next meeting.*

Unless everyone on the minutes' distribution list already knows the date of the next meeting (e.g., you meet every Monday morning), make sure you give the date of the next meeting or tell readers what actions must be completed before the next meeting date can be set.

10

Performance Appraisals

Corporate productivity is often linked to how corporations involve their employees in personal and corporate goals. One key to successful employee management is the performance appraisal.

Effective performance appraisals ensure that employees are working toward the same goals as their supervisors and, when they contain specific goals for the employee, help ensure the employee development required to meet future organizational needs.

Here are a few tips on planning and writing effective performance appraisals:

✔ **10-1.** *Plan carefully.*

Pull out last year's performance appraisal for each employee to review the work objectives that had been established. Add amendments to the appraisal form whenever the employee's work objectives are substantially modified.

✔ **10-2.** *Think long range.*

Think of the employee's performance over the whole year, not just the last month. Fight the tendency to be heavily influenced by recent events. Consider what the employee does better now than a year ago, as well as what he or she does well and should continue doing. Tell your employees: They'll appreciate that you noticed.

✔ **10-3.** *Think about the employee's whole job.*

Think about the employee's job as a whole—not just the adequacy of the person's technical and professional skills. Does the employee relate well to external as well as internal customers? What is the quality of the employee's written work? How well does this person work with others?

✔ **10-4.** *Be specific in your evaluation.*

"You're doing fine" doesn't tell employees what they're doing right or how to improve.

For the current year, set up an incident file to hold notes you make throughout the year about each employee's strengths and areas for improvement. Keep track of specific incidents of poor performance. Note times, dates, and discussions that took place. This way, when it comes time to write the appraisal, you'll be able to include details rather than just opinion.

✔ **10-5.** *Plan before writing.*

Before starting, gather and review for each employee:

☐ Position description

☐ Notes on performance you have made during the year

☐ Any performance standards

☐ Input from your manager or customers

☐ Performance appraisal form

✔ **10-6.** *Prepare for the interview by taking notes.*

Your notes should cover your major topics for each appraisal. They should also cover:

☐ Each person's top five to seven job responsibilities

☐ Each person's performance on major assignments, with specific examples; consider quality of work performed, on-time performance, job knowledge, initiative, and teamwork

✔ **10-7.** *Use the SMARTS criteria to create objectives.*

SMARTS refers to objectives that are:

Specific—clear and unambiguous

Measurable—have an observable outcome

Achievable—are realistic, given resources, control, and so on

Results-oriented—describe an outcome, not an activity

Timebound—offer specific completion dates

Supportive—tie an individual's objectives to organization's goals and objectives

✔ **10-8.** *Write negatives in an upbeat manner.*

Most statements that contain some negatives can be written in a positive way. For example, instead of writing, "Your problems stem from a lack of organization and improper management of your time," write "You need to improve your organizational and time management skills." With the first sentence, you sound as if you're getting ready to fire someone because of these "problems." In the revised sentence, you avoid writing that the employee has a "problem" and sound as if you're pointing the person in the direction of better future performance.

11

Status Reports

Here are 10 tips on organizing and writing status reports:

✔ **11-1.** *Organize the report to be scanned easily and in a way that highlights your accomplishments.*

Status reports are usually organized by project. Within each project are the accomplishments (completed tasks) and the ongoing jobs (pending). There should be some order to the projects (e.g., most important to least important, chronological, or numerical). Some status reports may highlight "key events" or "red flag items" first.

If you've worked on a particular project but didn't complete anything on it that week, don't start with that project, because it sets a negative tone. For example, one analyst's first subject stated: "The move of the FEP from Cluster 1 to Cluster 5 has been postponed due to the TPF implementation into PSS. The new implementation date is 4/11/95." Although this may be important information to pass along, you have not strictly speaking "accomplished" anything, so why lead with this item? When possible, lead with the projects you've accomplished the most with during the time covered in the report.

✔ **11-2.** *Write for one level above your supervisor as well as for your supervisor.*

We get sloppy when we write to a supervisor with whom we work closely every day. We don't orient the reader as to the scope of the project, nor are we precise in our rendering of what we accomplished. But remember that your supervisor will write his or her own status report based on yours and on your colleagues' reports. Therefore, try to write the report in such a way as to show what you've done, why you are doing it, and what its effect will be.

✔ **11-3.** *Think of your accomplishments in measurable, observable terms.*

Be alert to vague statements. An example: "Continued work on the interface from the gateway to the NAPLP emulator." What did you actually accomplish in measurable, observable terms? What part of the interface did you work on, and how far did you get? Did you spend 15 hours creating the interface, which is now complete? Then say so.

Active language is a helpful antidote to vagueness. Also, keeping paragraphs and sentences short helps you crystallize the "measurable, observable" heart of each of your thoughts.

✔ **11-4.** *Start accomplishments and pending items with verbs.*

It's easier to communicate what you've done if you begin each statement with a verb. Instead of writing "The modifications to the PARS outline submittal allocation process are completed," start with "Completed...."

✔ **11-5.** *Tell why you are working on a project.*

As your status report gets circulated, you want everyone to know not only *what* you did but *why* you did it. True, some of your readers may know this already. The ones who don't know, however, will be happy to see it.

For example, take this statement: "Implemented several modifications to the Railroad Commission production reports, correcting the reporting of skim oil volumes allocated from Acme's facilities." *Why* did you do this? What effect will it have on Acme? Your manager may know, but as your report goes upward, the "bottom line" of your actions will not be clear unless you underscore their contribution to the productivity and profitability of the department or organization.

✔ **11-6.** *Define acronyms and boil down jargon.*

Any chance that someone on your distribution list may not understand an acronym? If so, define it once and then use the acronym throughout the rest of your report. If you think of your reader's ease, not your own, you won't make the reader play guessing games.

✔ **11-7.** *Remind the reader of the estimated completion dates of ongoing projects.*

Don't write: "Work has begun on developing an archival and reloading process for PARS databases." Write: "Developing an archival and reloading process for PARS databases. Estimated completion date: June 15."

We know that you may be hesitant about promising an exact completion date. But any manager reading the word *developing* will automatically think: "When will it be done?" So, you can save a lot of time by giving an estimated completion date. It buys you some "wiggle room" but also adds a lot of measurable, observable reality to your report.

✔ **11-8.** *Come to the point quickly.*

If the status of each project under discussion takes more than 20 lines to describe, make sure that your first line doesn't just start detailing the background of the project but summarizes your forward movement. Ask yourself, "What's the news?" Start with the news, not with background details.

✔ **11-9.** *Use interesting graphic elements to help your reader follow your thoughts.*

Use headings that are ALL CAPITALS as well as **boldface**. Subheads can be upper and lowercase and underlined. Indent within headings to help your reader understand that the subheads belong within a heading.

Use bullets for a list of accomplishments, preferably in which each item starts with a verb.

✔ **11-10.** *Use an executive summary to give your reader an overview of your report.*

Unless your status report runs one page or less, use an "Executive Summary" to help you signal the reader about the highlights of what you're about to report.

In other words, try to pull together the chief ideas that cut across all the work you did on your projects, like this: "Continued work on six projects (name them) and began two new ones (name them). Although two problems were identified in Project ABC and Project DEF, we were able to find the logic error, correct the problem, and schedule implementation. Following a description of the status of each project, I've summarized miscellaneous activities as well as a few administrative matters."

12

Trip Reports

People take business trips for a variety of reasons: to become familiar with a division of the company, to meet new personnel, to promote new business, or to investigate problems at a plant. Whatever the reason for the trip, they usually need to document the trip upon their return. That's where the real problems begin.

Most people don't know what's expected of them in a trip report. Some people believe they should write down everything that happened while they were away, accounting for every minute spent while on the road. This way, they try to convey the impression that they weren't sloughing off while out of the office. Others get so involved with the technical issues they are reporting that they forget to focus on the purpose of the trip. Still others get so general that a supervisor reading the report would wonder why he or she'd ever sent the person in the first place.

To help guide you in writing effective trip reports, here are a few quick tips:

✔ **12-1.** *Don't lose sight of why you took the trip.*

Your company sent you somewhere so that you could accomplish something. Perhaps you were sent to make a sale or to evaluate a process or a piece of software that might benefit your department. In any case, in the first paragraph or two, remind the reader why you took the trip and give the highlights of what you discovered. Also, give a hint as to how your discoveries may benefit your department or organization.

Here are two examples of effective opening paragraphs:

> My familiarization trip to Distribution and the Harrison plant offered me insights into the production and distribution of our products, which in turn will help me sound more knowledgeable to our customers. In addition, I found that Distribution could increase its efficiency by adding a second system terminal.

> After viewing the automated autoclave systems of Thermal Equipment Corporation (TEC) and Applied Polymer Technology (APT), I recommend APT's system, especially if we implement a turnkey system.

✔ **12-2.** *Leave out some of the chatty tone and digressions.*

Just as if you were reporting on how you spent your summer vacation, you may tend to bring in a level of personal detail and reaction that is best kept to yourself. This applies to overly negative impressions of people and can also apply to any comment that really doesn't add weight to your ideas.

Here's how one person started his trip report:

> I would first like to start by thanking the company for giving me this fantastic opportunity....

Later, this same person makes the statement:

> As for my tour of the Harrison plant, it's almost too difficult to explain....

✔ **12-3.** *Don't gush! Show, don't tell.*

Although it's acceptable to sound enthusiastic, it's necessary to temper that enthusiasm with a realistic idea of the trip's purpose. Even in a familiarization report, you are usually expected to uncover something of importance—for example, a suggestion based on your observations or a problem you'd like to investigate.

Avoid phrases like "It's almost too hard to explain…"—a phrase that's more of an excuse than a valid observation. Also, eliminate phrases such as "I learned so much" (get specific) and "we had a great tour." Document what you saw and forget about adjectives.

✔ **12-4.** *Know when to use a chart, a table, or other graphics.*

Paragraphs are fine for most types of description, but if the heart of your report is to show a comparison or contrast, you may need to break away from prose and use a chart, a table, a graph, bullet points, or some other device designed to make your thoughts easy to comprehend.

One trip report writer compared two systems components and capabilities within paragraphs. The result: a hard-to-follow muddle. Here's how some of it sounded:

> TEC's computer hardware system was basically the same as our own Automated Cure Control System. Each autoclave was controlled by a Hewlett-Packard 220 or 310 microcomputer in the 9000 series. Hewlett-Packard's data acquisition unit model 9500 was used in most of the systems. The disk drive used was an HP 9000, which is a hard disk drive housed along with a floppy disk drive. There was, however, no central computer and no way for archiving data other than by floppy disk.

The comparison between two systems could be easier to grasp if it was laid out as a chart. Here's how some of that chart might look:

	TEC	**APT**
Autoclave control	Each one controlled by Hewlett-Packard 220 or 310 micro-computer	Two controlled by Hewlett-Packard 1000
Data acquisition unit	HP-3497A used for all autoclaves	HP-3497A used in each individual autoclave
Disk drive	Hard disk and floppy disks	Hard disk

✔ **12-5.** *Use a* Re *line to hold details of place, date, and purpose.*

A *Re* line in a trip report can help a busy reader focus instantly on the *what, where,* and *when* of your trip. Instead of starting to read the report, a reader can look at the *Re* line and get a mini overview of what is to be presented in the report. Here's an example:

Re: Oklahoma office visit March 16–20 to review and complete 1994 tax returns

PART 3

Promotional Writing

13

Advertisements

The following tips will help you sharpen your copywriting skills and create more effective promotions:

✔ **13-1.** *Orient every word to your reader.*

Copywriters know that the word *you* is the most important word in their vocabularies. By thinking of the reader's needs first, good copywriters never confuse their own biases or irrelevant sales points with appeals that will touch the lives of their audiences. An advertisement should underscore the benefits a reader gains by using a product or service.

✔ **13-2.** *Slogans help readers and listeners remember.*

"Pan Am makes the going great," "GE: We bring good things to life," and "American Express: Don't leave home without it" are examples of catchy slogans. These pithy phrases have permeated our minds, becoming part of a national idiom while reminding consumers of each company's spirit and services.

By using repeated slogans in ads and other sales literature, you provide a uniformity and unity to your promotions. Slogans not only help your customer remember you, they help form a single identifiable symbol in customers' minds.

✔ 13-3. *Carefully arrange your selling points.*

You must develop a feel for which points deserve top billing and which are added attractions. For example, a typing service may use perfect typing as a major sales point, choosing to mention it before the phrase "24 hours a day." To help readers absorb more than a few sales points, you may wish to use bullets, numbers, or subheads.

✔ 13-4. *Avoid sexism.*

When you reach for a phrase like "an advertising man's job," an alarm should sound in your brain. "An advertising professional's job" is more generic, since the field isn't limited to males, and should be used unless you are describing a particular male. "Ad man" is one of a storehouse of stock phrases that now must be rethought and reworded.

✔ 13-5. *Be tasteful.*

No one can teach you about taste: You either have it or you don't. But you can become more sensitive to exactly what constitutes bad taste by studying the ads you see all around you.

We once saw an ad for a beautician specializing in electrolysis. The ad featured a line drawing of a ballet dancer in a spotlight. The copy read, "Why share the spotlight with unwanted hair?" Something about hair in the spotlight struck us as unfortunate—the kind of image you want to forget, not remember.

✔ **13-6.** *Use graphics.*

Don't be dissuaded from using graphics. Photographs, line drawings, charts, maps, tables, and other illustrations attract the reader. Graphics should be of high quality and should blend harmoniously with the body copy. Don't just use a graphic because it's handy or free: Use it when it will communicate an idea well.

✔ **13-7.** *Avoid jargon.*

Advertisements and promotions about technical products may require the use of technical terms. Indeed, technical terms such as *CPU, binomial theorem,* or *biodegradable* seem hard to avoid under such circumstances. What you should avoid are the terms and catch phrases (e.g., rack and pinion steering) that only people in the field can readily define.

✔ **13-8.** *Keep sentences and paragraphs short.*

People are scared off by lengthy sentences and paragraphs; they view them with the trepidation with which a light eater views a 12-ounce sirloin. The words seem to blend into a formidable chunk of type. The solution? Loosen it up. Break up lengthy sentences and paragraphs. Allow the reader to grasp your message in short, easy-to-understand blocks.

✔ **13-9.** *Don't forget the obvious.*

Sometimes you're so busy reeling off sales points in an ad that you forget to state the obvious. You may remember to put in the phone number—but leave out the area code! You may tell readers where and when a seminar will be held—but forget to mention the cost!

✔ **13-10.** *Add an additional inducement.*

Just as a *P.S.* adds an additional thought to a letter, a flyer or ad is sometimes enhanced by a bonus sales point, another reason to buy the product or service. On a TV commercial for various kitchen appliances, a voice excitedly tacks on, "And if you act now, you'll receive, free of charge...." These added inducements do tip the scales in favor of the sale.

14

Brochures

Here are eleven tips that will help you create more effective brochures:

✔ **14-1.** *Make sure the cover tells your story.*

The front panel or page is the first thing that your customer sees. That cover should communicate the basics of what you're selling (or else be so attention getting that it compels the reader to read on). This need not be an elaborate explanation of what you are offering, but simply a statement of what you do. A barber shop has a barber's pole, a doctor may have a sign on the door identifying his or her practice. Similarly, a brochure should state your business or purpose. It can be terse (e.g., "career counseling," "membership application" or "how to survive a hotel fire"), but it should be there.

✔ **14-2.** *Let the quality of the sales piece suit its purpose and audience.*

Although a sales piece should always look neat and clean, it need not always be printed on fine paper stock or illustrated with photographs. These decisions depend on the nature of your business and on your audience.

A slick catalog may well be needed to sell fancy gift items, but a slim, serviceable black and white catalog may be all that's required to sell inexpensive "how-to" managerial reports. Why? Because some catalogs and brochures are "selling" status and glamour in addition to the product or service, whereas other brochures or catalogs are selling more utilitarian items.

✔ **14-3.** *Acquaint the reader with your service or product.*

One of the purposes of sales literature is to establish common ground with prospects—telling them who you are and what you have to offer. A brochure's cover or front panel may communicate this information, but you may need to spend a few lines of copy describing specifically what you do. The brochure for a service called *PR Newswire* devotes several pages to communicating just how the newswire helps businesspeople reach the media.

✔ **14-4.** *Don't promise what you can't deliver.*

Without lying and without exaggeration, you can produce a brochure that is impressive. If you're a one-person business, you can create a brochure that gives the impression that you're a medium-size business. But don't lie. Keep your brochure defensible. Never list clients you don't have or products you are not ready to deliver.

✔ **14-5.** *Make benefits meaningful to customers.*

A charming New England inn sells coziness, and its brochure must emphasize a fireplace, down quilt, sleigh rides, or hot mulled cider. These features translate into customer benefits such as escape, relaxation, sound sleep, and serenity.

Put yourself in the reader's position. Does the reader

have children? Then, perhaps, some of the inn's photographs should show children at play, safely supervised and not under foot.

✔ **14-6.** *Keep a uniform look in all your literature.*

Not everyone can afford to furnish a living room or bedroom all at once; people are often forced to settle for a more random, less "together" look—at least until they can afford to give some consideration to how well things match. With sales literature, the advantage of maintaining a similar graphic look is not just uniformity but achieving a cumulative impression on potential customers.

By seeing the same logo, the same typeface, the same paper stock, and even the same packaging, customers develop a Pavlovlike response to your product or service before they even see the name of your company.

✔ **14-7.** *Always put informative captions on photographs.*

Research indicates that photos capture our interest, so that we're likely to look at a photo in a brochure before—and even instead of—reading the copy. Since people are drawn to photos, they read captions. Therefore, make sure your captions are informative and highlight the benefits of what you are selling. In other words, don't just identify the photo as a tennis court ("26 lighted courts") or pool ("Olympic size pool"); tell people about the benefits of each facility ("Play whenever you like, day or evening"; "Take a refreshing dip...or swim laps in your own private lane").

✔ **14-8.** *Let the copy run as long as necessary.*

Although brevity is usually a plus, there are times when readers want to know all the details included in a lengthy sales piece. You should be concise, but you should also include all the important information. Generally, when you're selling an expensive product or service, like a condominium, car, or photocopier, you may have to write lengthy copy to be comprehensive and persuasive.

✔ **14-9.** *Don't rush!*

Creating excellent brochures sometimes takes days of meticulous detail work. It involves checking and rechecking the work of copywriters, designers, and printers. It means deciding whether to use photos, and, if so, which photos to use and when reshooting a photo may be required. A good phrase, a fine photo, the right paper stock, the appropriate typeface—they may be worth the wait.

✔ **14-10.** *Make your brochure worth keeping.*

If your brochure tells people something they don't know or something they feel is practical, they may want to keep it around for a while. Try to find ways to make your brochure the type of piece that people will want to keep.

Whether your brochure gives tips on tying ties or on packing UPS packages securely, try to make the brochure valuable to the potential customer. I once developed a brochure for a travel agent. The panel provided solid information on how to get the most out of using a travel agent. The travel agent's clients tended to keep the brochure because they found themselves going back to the tips on using travel agents effectively.

✔ **14-11.** *Tell the reader what to do next.*

A brochure should not leave the reader hanging. Generally, it should lead the reader to take action or at least lead to a telephone number to call or to an address where you can be reached. In many cases, catalogs, brochures, or flyers will request an order or tell you how to proceed. They provide everything necessary for motivating you to complete the action.

A brochure might contain a coupon for the reader to use in responding. The final line of many sales brochures asks the reader to write, to call, to send for more information, to enclose a check—direct action. Brochures and catalogs usually can't afford to be vague about how the sale will be consummated. Generally speaking, sales literature should spell out exactly what the reader has to do to obtain the product or service.

15

Direct Mail

"How can I make my direct mail more effective?" I hear this question a lot in my business writing seminars. Getting people to buy your products and services through the mail has got to be one of the most challenging communication situations in the business world and one that we face every day. Here are twenty tips that I believe will help increase response:

✔ **15-1.** *Personalize your mailer.*

People love to weed out third-class mail before getting to the good stuff. In large companies, the mail room or a secretary is on the lookout for any mail that doesn't look like it's a welcomed message. So, make your direct mail look as much like a piece of personal correspondence as possible:

- ☐ Avoid labels and ink jets. If your mailing is small enough, type the envelopes. If large, use a daisy wheel printer.
- ☐ Use real stamps rather than an indicia or metered postage.
- ☐ Use your own name instead of a company name.

✔ **15-2.** *Use testimonials.*

If you've received letters praising your product or services, use them in your direct-mail letter. If you don't have testimonials, solicit them from satisfied customers.

✔ **15-3.** *Keep postage low by lightening up your package.*

Try to stay with letter-size pieces: 3 ounces or less, no thicker than 0.25", and smaller than 6.125" × 11.5".

You may not need the fancy paper you've been using. After all, do your recipients care about 60-lb stock paper? Test by sending some light paper to some people and heavy stock to others. If the results are the same, use the lighter paper stock.

✔ **15-4.** *Use specific, concrete terms rather than vague generalities.*

Quality, service, value, and *convenience* all sound nice, but what do they really mean? If a service or product can save a customer money, tell how. Use value comparisons readers can picture (e.g., two for the price of one).

✔ **15-5.** *Avoid* truthfully, honestly, *and* I'll be honest with you.

You don't have to be a Harvard psychologist to know that these phrases may call into question the truthfulness of other parts of your message. It's as if you're saying, "I'm being honest this time—no kidding!"

✔ **15-6.** *Use reliable motivators.*

Fear. Guilt. Exclusivity. Greed. These are the things that sway us, the motivating factors that lie behind a great deal of seemingly mysterious human behavior.

Take fear for example. If you're selling financial services, you may sway people by focusing them on the natural fear that we all have—that we'll be penniless when we get to retirement age! Your pitch can conjure up the fear of not having enough money for retirement as a way of introducing your service or product. Fear is a real emotion, and direct-mail writers know that to exploit fear you must not be afraid to be graphic, specific, and startling.

✔ **15-7.** *Use emotional words instead of intellectual ones.*

For example, "This is to notify you that you have been selected to participate..." or "I'm writing to you about an exceptional opportunity that exists for you right now." The second phrase is better because it speaks to you—personally, openly, emotionally.

Eliminate conditional statements (e.g., *would* or *could*)—they register as negative. Stay away from *strictly, stringently,* and *severely* ("Our supply is severely limited").

✔ **15-8.** *Make sure your copy shows a benefit for the reader.*

People are interested in themselves. Direct-mail pitches must keep the reader's benefit in mind. Some words and phrases that help you do this are *opportunity, free, easy, for you, you pay only, you'll be able to, private invitation to.*

The old advertising adage, "Sell the sizzle, not the steak," is true. A steak is, after all, a piece of beef. But, the sizzle of a steak on a barbecue grill on the fourth of July—well, that's America. Get the idea?

✔ **15-9.** *Ask a provocative question.*

According to direct-mail consultant Bob Bly, questions in direct-mail pieces should arouse the reader's curiosity, deal with timely or important issues, or ask something to which the reader really wants an answer.

"If you were to find out today that you had only a short time to live, would you feel comfortable with the amount of life insurance that you have provided for your family?" That's how United of Omaha starts a direct-mail piece— and it is a riveting approach.

✔ **15-10.** *Be honest.*

George Washington might have been discussing direct mail when he said: "Honesty is the best policy." A leading market research bureau asked people what they disliked most about direct mail: 41 percent answered "deception."

People can tell when you're lying. A classic example of a direct-mail lie is when the outside of the direct-mail piece's envelope is marked *personal and confidential,* but the salutation of the letter reads *Gentlemen.*

✔ **15-11.** *Use a provocative quotation in your headline.*

Provocative questions engage readers by forcing them to compose an answer. That involves thought. If you have them ponder the right question, you are beginning to control—or influence—their thought process.

✔ **15-12.** *Make your offer in the first few paragraphs.*

Consultant Bob Bly gives an example of a first-paragraph offer made by 3M Systems for creating color slides and overhead transparencies: "Our free brochure tells you how you can make sophisticated slides and overhead transparencies...over the *phone,* in *minutes.*"

✔ **15-13.** *Pay attention to the graphic appearance of a sales letter.*

How a letter looks can be almost as important as what it says. That's why you need to be sensitive to format issues such as spacing, use of bulleted items, boldface, and subheads.

✔ **15-14.** *Decide whether your goal is to generate leads or to make the sale.*

Before you write, you need to know if your piece is meant to generate leads or to actually sell goods and services immediately. Most direct mail tries to uncover leads which then lead to sales.

Lead-generating letters should be short. After all, if you tell too much, you won't have anything new to send to your prospective client. Then, to generate sales, you need to tell the whole story in your follow-up material. Readers associate longer letters with honesty.

✔ **15-15.** *Use the sales sequence to add persuasion to your message.*

Stuck on how to organize your persuasive pitch letter? Think of this handy five-step sequence:

□ Gain attention

□ Show a need

□ Satisfy the need

□ Show benefits

□ Call for action

✔ **15-16.** *Avoid contradictions.*

Your language must be consistent or you'll stop readers in their tracks. This is an example of inconsistency:

Dear Gourmet,

You may never again have to worry about time for cooking....

Gourmets enjoy cooking and don't worry about saving time!

Or take this example: "This nostalgic new series of...." *Nostalgic* plays on the old; *new* is just that.

✔ 15-17. *If you make a claim, prove it.*

It's difficult to prove that something has quality because *quality* is a nebulous term. *Popular* is a good word to use if you can back it up with statistics (e.g., "Our popular catalog has been requested by more than 5000 businesspeople from around the world").

✔ 15-18. *Target your audience.*

A targeted approach narrows your pitch to fit a specific audience. In a pitch to neighboring towns, one management consultant mentioned clients from the surrounding area, thus ensuring that his target audience would be aware that he is "in the neighborhood."

✔ 15-19. *Test all your letters and keep track of responses.*

To survive in direct mail, you must test. Why? Because if you are not getting adequate response, you must change your approach. If you are getting good results, maybe you could even improve on those results.

✔ 15-20. *Know the rules of "fear."*

There are three rules to follow when using fear as a motivator:

1. Make sure the reader knows that you have a solution to his or her problem.

2. Write a direct challenge, not a "what-if" subjunctive (e.g., "What will you do when..." rather than "What would you do if...").

3. Don't lose your nerve halfway through and start to inject light-heartedness. Maintain a consistent tone to avoid undercutting your impact on your reader.

16

Press Releases

What do journalists want? It's an age-old question, and answers will vary from medium to medium, and journalist to journalist. Here are a few touchstones that you should consider before you get ready to distribute your release:

1. Is the story unique? What makes the story one of a kind? Is it compelling? Universal? Ask yourself: Who cares about this? If someone was pitching the story to you, would someone besides yourself or your client care? The story has to make others care. If the story is pointless, puffery, or overstated, it won't get used.

2. Is the story part of a trend? Can you link your story or new product with other stories in the media that show the direction of the economy or of society in general? After the Clarence Thomas Senate hearings, media used a spate of stories about sexual harassment simply because the Thomas hearings opened the door to the media's receptiveness for more information about the problem of sexual harassment.

   Recently, we wanted to get publicity for some national tests we had devised to measure students' overall skill in punctuation and grammar. Although the tests may be newsworthy because they are new and because they speak to a universal problem, the story is more special if it fits into a larger trend.

The trend we fit it into was one of the average student's lack of skills in history and geography. There had been well-publicized stories about the average high school student being unable to find Japan on a map or to tell, within 50 years, when the Civil War was fought. We used these two examples as a lead-in to the question, "How would 'Johnny' do if he took a battery of tests on punctuation and grammar?"

A story about how your company is conforming to the American Disabilities Act may not, in itself, be newsworthy, but if it can be part of a story about what several local companies are doing to conform to the act, it will have more appeal.

Some columnists look for stories that are not "news" but are events that link up with other events. Sometimes your release can get picked up because a journalist sees it as fitting into a larger framework. I once sent a release about poor business writing to a columnist. Along with the release, I enclosed a copy of my "Sexist Terms" poster. The journalist wound up interviewing me for a column about sexual harassment.

(Tip: Be careful about trying to get too much mileage out of an old story by rehashing it in a new release.)

3. Does the story have humor? Humor is appreciated and can be used to entice the media. The media love quirky stories about people or organizations marching to the sound of a different drummer. We used humor to attract the media to a story we created about the decline of considerate behavior in America. We created an "Association of Victims of the Functionally Inconsiderate" and even made up a word for the new wave of inconsiderate behavior—*Inconsideracy*. We then created a poster: "Ten Traits of the Functionally Inconsiderate" and made sure that those traits were so

universal that they'd bring a smile to one's face (e.g., "Functionally inconsiderate people bring a week's worth of groceries to the '10 items or less' line at the supermarket"). The story was picked up by Gannett and ran throughout the United States and Canada.

4. Is there a twist? If a story isn't unique, it can at least have an unusual twist that merits attention. Show flair, show broad appeal, show enthusiasm. For example, a story about touring Paris is a travel cliché, but a story about touring Paris's sewer system has an interesting twist. A story about a walking club is routine, but a story about a walking club in which all the walkers are over 80 years old has a clever twist. At *Newsday*, one way the business editor measures the appeal of a story is to ask: "Could a taxi driver pick up the paper, look at the story and think, "Wow! That's really interesting!"?

Writing the Release

✔ **16-1.** *Always include a contact person and date on your release.*

Journalists shouldn't struggle to find out who to call. The name of your release's contact person should be in the upper right corner of the release, followed by that person's phone number. If you can provide an evening or weekend number, that's even better. Some journalists would prefer to have the name of someone involved in the story as well as the name and phone number of a PR contact. If there's a story at a local company, many journalists prefer you to list the contact at the company rather than the person at an outside PR firm. Don't take offense: The important thing is to get the media to express interest in the story.

The worst thing you can do is to put down the name and phone number of a contact person who is not usually available or who has no intimate knowledge of the story.

When the media call, you have to be ready: You may not get a second chance.

Since press releases tend to pile up on desks, you need to include a date on your release. The popular phrase, "For immediate release" has become a press release convention and neither helps nor hinders your release in being picked up by the media.

✔ **16-2.** *Avoid misspellings.*

Mistakes and misspellings may not disqualify a release from consideration, but they do undermine it. One real estate writer once got a press release addressed to the "Reality Editor." Misspelling an editor's name is almost a sure way of having your release dumped in what the British call "File 13."

One press release from a California PR firm referred to a company based in "Hodge Podge," which we on Long Island call Hauppauge! This release was never used at *Newsday*, but it did get lots of laughs for the months it was posted on the bulletin board.

✔ **16-3.** *Beware of acronyms and jargon.*

No one appreciates a release teeming with obscure acronyms or even too many popular ones such as LAN, IPO, DOS, HIV, or GOP. And no one likes to read a release loaded with the jargon of a particular field such as medicine, data processing, or publishing.

Paul Schreiber, who writes the "Doing Business" column at *New York Newsday*, tells this story of a maker of IBM-compatible equipment who sent a release to him. The release reads

> I-data has announced two products to take the headaches out of Advanced Function Printing (AFP) for users of IBM 3270 mainframes. The ida820 HP AFP

brings IBM 3820 compatibility to Hewlett-Packard LaserJet printers, while the 820n Remote Print Package (RPP) uses a PS/2 workstation and the ida820 HP AFP software to speed AFP output time.

Says Schreiber, "'I-data' needs to take the headaches out of that."

✔ **16-4.** *Don't overkill.*

Avoid hype words like *leading, enhanced, unique, significant, powerful, innovative,* and *advanced.*

✔ **16-5.** *Include the who, what, where, how, when, and why of the story.*

Before sending out your release, check to see that you've answered these primary questions—early in your release.

Sending the Release

✔ **16-6.** *Don't use the shotgun approach.*

People who send releases to the media are split over the issue of sending releases to more than one person at a particular newspaper or magazine.

Some argue that there's safety in numbers or that the more people who read the release, the better chance you have that someone will take an interest in it. But that's fuzzy thinking. Journalists usually feel that the "shotgun" approach is off-putting because a reporter who feels she or he is one of many people getting the release may think, "let someone else do the story." If you pitch a specific story to a specific reporter, you may make up in quality what you lose in quantity.

To find out who the right person is to send your story to, read the magazine or newspaper for a while and look at the bylines. Pretty soon you'll discern the person who most often tackles stories like the one you want to pitch.

If you decide to send a release to two journalists at the same newspaper, magazine, or radio station, indicate that you are sending it to several areas. Then, the journalists don't trip over trying to find out how many others at the same organization may be thinking about working on the story.

✔ **16-7.** *Keep current about journalists and media.*

Journalists have been known to receive press releases addressed to their predecessors years after the predecessor's demise or replacement. One editor told me he still received press releases addressed to a predecessor who had been dead for 18 years. Therefore, you have to stay on top of who is handling a particular beat at a newspaper or magazine.

Also, you need to know the latest trends or directions at certain media, since newspapers and magazines are always changing with the times. You should also make note of the differences between the wire services so you don't waste any of your releases. For example, you might choose Knight Ridder to send a release to if that release was breaking news about the financial world, but they are less likely to run a feature story than, say, Gannett's newswire.

In contrast, *Crain's New York Business* (circulation of 80,000) is more likely to pick up a story about an unusual New York City small business than would national business magazines such as *Forbes* or *Fortune*.

✔ **16-8.** *Don't be too cute.*

Some releases have been sent in bottles, tubes, tins, balloons, and occasionally, with a gift. Gimmicks rarely work; gifts are returned.

✔ **16-9.** *Send photos only when appropriate.*

According to Paul Schreiber of *Newsday*, "Trade publications use product shots and weeklies don't mind groundbreakings, but big papers usually take their own photographs."

Following Up

✔ **16-10.** *Know when to call for follow-up.*

Newspaper people are usually on deadline late in the afternoon, so avoid calling after 4 p.m. The earlier in the day you call, the better. Try at 11 a.m. when the journalist has had some coffee and may be mulling over which stories to work on.

As for sending a note instead of calling, you may gain points for politeness, but you also risk having your follow-up note get buried under a pile of press releases.

Many journalists resent follow-ups because they think "the story won't get lost if I'm interested." However, human nature being what it is, you may want to check back with people every month or two just to make sure.

Journalists may complain that "if everyone who sent us a release followed up, we'd never get a chance to do any writing." True, but if "the squeaky wheel gets the grease," aren't you upping the chances of getting some attention if you're willing to follow up?

✔ **16-11.** *When following up, don't just ask, "Did you receive my release?"*

Be prepared to talk about angles that could make the release of interest to the writer's readers. It's silly to ask if the release was received because most mail is received—if you give it a reasonable amount of time to get there (two weeks).

✔ **16-12.** *For breaking news, use the phone.*

Sometimes you do have a noteworthy story of local or national interest (e.g., the death of the CEO of a large local company, winning a large contract). In these cases, call the editor and then fax the story over. But breaking news is different from a feature story. Don't try to add immediacy to a feature by sending it to the editor FedEx. A lot of dull stories sent by overnight mail simply get thrown out. Journalists suggest that PR people use newswire services (e.g., PR Newswire) for breaking stories.

✔ **16-13.** *Use appropriate phrases.*

Nothing turns off a journalist more than when a PR person calls up to "place" a story. You don't "place" stories; newspapers don't exist for PR people to call in their renditions of the news. And avoid the great temptation to tell editors that your story is "perfect" for their readers. The editors will be the judges of that.

17

Telemarketing Scripts

By the year 2000, most sales will take place over the telephone. We live in an era of telemarketing, of catalogs, of shop-at-home.

But when you call a person at home, you are competing with dozens of distractions—the demands of housekeeping, children, meals, leisure activities, paying bills. In other words, if you intend to sell a product or service by telephone, you must be good at catching—and holding—a person's attention, sounding like a human being (not a script), and closing the sale.

Obviously, the actual words or script a caller uses on the telephone is only one of many factors (e.g., list segmentation, general telephone etiquette, voice, training, ability to respond to questions) that will determine telemarketing success. My quick tips, however, will focus solely on stylistic issues involving the organization, wording, and phrasing of the script.

✔ **17-1.** *Be prepared to depart from the script.*

Be prepared for all possible inquiries about the product or service—including unexpected questions about pricing, delivery, taxes, postage, and warranties.

Adjust your script, if necessary, for the hour, day, or season of the call or, if applicable, to new rates, special price advantages, or special circumstances.

✔ **17-2.** *Be ready to deal with the public—and their quirks.*

Be ready to change the script to adapt to the feedback you receive from a potential customer. Be polite, never sarcastic. Be your pleasant, businesslike self.

✔ **17-3.** *Ask yourself hard questions about what you are selling.*

As you plan and write your script, focus on the key factors in the sale and ask yourself a few questions:

☐ Who is the prospect?

☐ Has the prospect heard of my product or service?

☐ What is the chief benefit of my product or service to my caller?

☐ How much does my prospect know about my product or service?

☐ How much information will it take to be convincing?

✔ **17-4.** *Identify yourself quickly.*

The phone rings. You pick it up. The voice at the other end says: "Hello, I'm calling from MCI. May I ask you a few questions about your long-distance service? What long distance are you currently using?"

The opening is standard: a greeting ("Hello"), a quick identification ("I'm calling from..."), and an immediate question ("What long-distance service...?"). Most people are polite enough to indulge a caller for a moment or two.

And the first few moments are almost up, so the sale must begin soon.

✔ 17-5. *Open a "wedge."*

The next few words spoken by the telemarketer are critical. The phone company, after finding that you are using its competitor's service, now has the opening wedge it needs. "How much do you spend on average each month making long-distance calls?"

Some people may show reluctance at this point—people don't like to share their spending habits with strangers on the telephone. They may even think that the IRS is making the call!

✔ 17-6. *Make your offer.*

When you start to get a few details about the prospect's current situation (obviously an inadequate one—after all, the prospect is in the hands of your competitor), you can make your offer. The phone company does this by asking a rhetorical question—"Would you be interested in saving money on your long-distance calls?"

Now there's a question that's loaded. Would anyone ever answer it: "No, I enjoy paying top dollar for phone service!"

✔ 17-7. *Be prepared to deal with "no sale."*

At this point, the prospect may truly engage in a conversation about your service or may beg off by saying "Send me some literature" or "I've got to go—a call is coming in on 'call waiting'" or "I have to get back to the dinner table."

Although many telemarketers expect to close a high rate of prospects on the phone, the rate will depend in part on the expense and complexity of your offering. With higher-priced products (long-distance service), the caller should expect a prospect to ask for literature so that the prospect can make a more leisurely, informed decision rather than be rushed into a decision on a single telephone call.

✔ **17-8.** *Try to keep the conversation moving forward.*

Your telemarketing script really begins with a joining of hands with the prospect, a description of how you'll save the prospect money.

At this stage in the script, you may design a series of questions aimed at ferreting out the prospect's unique situation as a long-distance user: "When do you make most of your calls?" Naturally, the telemarketer must be prepared for all possible answers like "in the morning," "on weekends," "after midnight," or "between 3 a.m. and 4 a.m."

✔ **17-9.** *Follow up on what you learn.*

The follow-up to a long-distance caller's answer like "during business hours" might be: "Then, Mr. Jones, is it fair to say that most of the money you spend on monthly long-distance calls is spent on weekdays between 9 a.m. and 5 p.m.?"

The telemarketer simply reflects the information heard from the prospect and, at the same time, moves toward a specific comparison that is tailored to the prospect's specific long-distance needs.

✔ **17-10.** *Be prepared to have the prospect go off on a tangent.*

Since people are human, they will often pepper their conversation with random thoughts, jokes, wishes, flashes of anger, and irrelevancies from their current life situation. They may tell you about their unhappy marriage or that they are missing their favorite TV program or that they hate their mother-in-law.

Now it's time to focus the caller on the results of your questioning: "What it all comes down to, Mr. Jones, is that by day you could be saving $25 on your calls and another $15 per month on the calls you make in the evening."

If the caller likes to yammer away to a friend in Brisbane, Winnipeg, or Lyon, you can suggest a "special plan" and save them even more money: "By using our international service, you'd receive an additional 10 percent savings...."

✔ **17-11.** *Dramatize the benefits.*

Now, you need to walk the reader through an easy-to-follow scenario of how these savings will take place once the caller becomes a customer: Our long-distance telemarketer might say, "How that works for you is that every time you make an international call...." The key word is *you*. It's the most persuasive word in the language. You can't use it enough in either telemarketing or in sales writing.

✔ **17-12.** *Sell convenience as well as savings.*

Lest you think that money is the only motivating factor in a telemarketing sale, the phone company, smelling blood, begins to harp on the fact that the competing phone company sends you two bills—with the telemarketer's phone service, you'll get only one bill. (Receiving two bills is a monumental annoyance but, for most of us, it would not be a prime motivating reason to switch. But it could clinch the sale.)

✔ **17-13.** *Move toward closing the sale.*

Tell the prospect what will now happen to bring the promises made in the call to fruition: "In about eight days, you'll receive a package detailing how you'll save...." By the time the prospect has agreed to receive the package, the caller has probably also found out which states the prospect calls most frequently, how much money the prospect spends on international calls monthly, and which countries the prospect calls most frequently. Now, the telemarketer can hand that information over to whoever prepares the package to be sent to the prospect. The more you know about a potential customer, the easier it will be to meet his or her needs.

✔ **17-14.** *Let your script reflect your best telephone technique.*

Use the customer's name frequently in the script and during the call. People like the sound of their own names; by consciously using a person's name, the caller establishes a personal quality to the call.

Repeat vital information. Always check spellings of names; recheck the amount, type, and product numbers of anything ordered. Have the customer spell out unusual street, city, or locality names. Double-check telephone numbers, credit card numbers, and order confirmation numbers.

18

Newsletters

With more than 25,000 active newsletters, *The Wall Street Journal* pronounced newsletter publishing one of the fastest growing industries in the United States. Newsletters are tied to the knowledge explosion. Specific clients want specific information. If you have it, then this becomes an effective means to reach your client.

Although a well-run newsletter can turn a 50 percent profit, about half the start-ups fail—because publishers either overestimate reader interest or underestimate costs. The first-year cost of starting typical business newsletters that provide trade news in a specific area is about $50,000.

There are two basic types of newsletter: subscription and promotional. Most entrepreneurs use promotional newsletters that are free or low-cost and that are used as a marketing tool rather than to produce revenue.

Many organizations publish promotional newsletters that they distribute free to customers, clients, prospects, employees, journal editors, and decision makers in their industries.

Newsletters do not tend to generate leads or sales. Rather, they help you build your image and reputation with a select group of prospects (those who receive the newsletter) over time.

The following are tips on writing better newsletters:

✔ **18-1.** *Choose a simple readable format, typeface, and type size.*

Most newsletter formats are simple. All that's needed is a clear layout, a title and date, and headlines to introduce the stories. There is no set form. The simplest newsletters are typewritten and offset: They are often no more than two sides of a single 8½-by-11" piece of paper.

The newsletter's look should match its intended audience. Typewritten newsletters are fine when the information presented is vital. But sometimes, image may be as important as the information itself. If your business is concerned with image, it may pay to make your newsletter graphically distinctive and to spend money reproducing the information on fine bond paper or on a heavy, glossy paper. In any case, let an outside consultant, agency, or designer lay out your first issue and help you to choose typefaces, paper stock, and ink colors. You need to be sensitive to these elements because they all form an impression on the reader.

Establish a recognizable format and stick to it so readers can become comfortable with the content as well as find information simply and quickly.

Make sure a professional communicator, either an in-house staff person or an external consultant, is charged with the responsibility of producing the newsletter.

✔ **18-2.** *Keep the newsletter—and the stories in it—brief.*

Stories in a newsletter can range from a single paragraph to several pages, but most are shorter rather than longer. Unlike a brochure, in which each section builds on the previous section, each article in a newsletter is self-contained. Consequently, the order of articles is not particularly important. Common sense dictates that you put the most important and interesting stories on page 1 and other copy on the inside pages.

✔ **18-3.** *Let your resources—and your readers' needs—determine how often you publish.*

Obviously publication schedules will vary from newsletter to newsletter. If your newsletter comes out too frequently, you are putting great demands on your time; if it comes out too infrequently, people may forget you're in business! You can publish every month or every other month, or twice a year. But don't publish an issue if you have nothing new to say: It's better to postpone the issue until there is real news to report. The reader will forgive a late issue but will not continue to read a newsletter that contains nothing of real value.

✔ **18-4.** *Keep articles and tips focused on the readers' interests.*

Don't try to be everything to everybody. People are interested in self-help and in discovering information that will be useful, profitable, or interesting. Newsletters shouldn't wander too far from providing this type of help. For example, a whole issue of *PR Ink* is devoted to "How to Pick Press Kit Photos Editors Will Want to Use." This topic is of interest to its readers, PR people at small firms who are constantly sending press releases to the media.

The New York Metro division of the American Society of Training and Development publishes a newsletter, *Lamplighter,* with articles of interest to human resource managers, training managers, and personnel managers. No wonder, then, that an article such as "Conflict Can Be Positive" (November 1992 issue) could be of interest to almost every subscriber.

A newsletter titled the *Information Systems Writer* targets systems professionals who must write a great deal on the job. Two of its typical articles are titled: "What Computer Software Can't Teach You about Writing," and "Proposals: How to Make Headlines Sell Your Ideas."

Don't preach to the readership. In other words, the newsletter shouldn't exist simply to sell products to customers or a management line to employees. Instead, its purpose should be to educate and stimulate a genuine dialogue between you and your audience.

Don't ignore or exclude bad news. To establish your credibility, include any problems and what action is being taken to solve them.

✔ **18-5.** *Be informal and relaxed.*

Your newsletter's articles should have the warmth and tone of the human voice. Write to express—not to impress. Use words that communicate your message clearly and concretely. Don't use any of the lawyerlike language that is often found in business communication (e.g., *herein, wherein, heretofore, deem it necessary*). Stay away from too much passive language (e.g., *It is recommended, It is believed*). Feel free to use contractions to warm up your prose. Use short sentences and short paragraphs. We don't want you to use slang, but you can get away with an occasional colloquialism. Some sentences can begin with conjunctions. You can, when appropriate, use *I* or *We* and probably get away with the occasional exclamation point. You can use dashes liberally, underline or italicize text, and even lean on the occasional parenthetical remark.

✔ **18-6.** *Let your audience determine the price of your newsletter.*

Newsletter subscription prices vary widely. Many newsletters are free or charge a nominal amount: $20–$50 per year. Others cost many hundreds of dollars, providing immediate, insider advice in prominent industries. Here are the titles of several newsletters followed by their annual subscription costs:

Motorcycle Business Newsletter, twice monthly, $96

Aerospace Daily, daily, $520

The Computer Marketing Newsletter, monthly, $60

Speechwriter's Newsletter, twice monthly, $82

The Food & Drug Letter, biweekly, $335

Adoption Report, quarterly, $5

Many newsletters are promotional and therefore are not operated for profit. Sometimes they are published by nonprofit organizations or those using newsletters as marketing tools. Interestingly, some newsletters that began as free publications have become income producers.

The purpose of charging a nominal fee for a newsletter is not entirely for the purpose of defraying its actual costs—even the most modest newsletter represents several dollars a year cost per recipient for production costs alone, without counting your own time and labor. However, people tend to value things by what they cost, so that they tend to regard a free newsletter as being nothing more than pure advertising literature. In fact, if you do intend to distribute your newsletter free, in the interest of getting wide circulation (at least initially), it is a wise move to inscribe an annual subscription fee on the masthead, whether or not you actually charge subscribers.

✔ 18-7. *Vary typefaces.*

Although serif typefaces are more readable than sans serif faces, you need not limit yourself to one or the other. For contrast, you may use sans serif faces in "Question & Answer" sections of articles as well as in "For More Information" paragraphs highlighting listings of addresses and telephone numbers of additional sources. The typeface for your logo can be as conservative or as jazzy as you see fit as long as its "look" matches the expectations of a typical reader. Obviously a PR newsletter can be more starkly dramatic in its graphics than a newsletter devoted to investments, training, or systems.

Readers demand larger and more legible typefaces, so by cutting back on article length and by making the typeface larger, you may actually be able to communicate more to your readers.

✔ **18-8.** *Get feedback from your readers.*

Plan to systematically assess the success or failure of your newsletter. If you don't, you will receive complaints, but you won't know how many readers were pleased or how many didn't even read the newsletter.

One method is to include a survey as part of each newsletter. By designing the questionnaire well, you'll encourage people to respond. Leave opportunity for open-ended responses, including suggestions. These may provide you with a multitude of creative ideas. Here are some questions you might pose:

1. How much of the newsletter do you usually read?
2. How informative do you find the newsletter?
3. How up-to-date do you find the newsletter?
4. How much help does the newsletter give you in doing your job better?
5. How attractive and easy-to-read is the format?
6. How often should the newsletter be published?
7. What suggestions do you have to make the newsletter better?

By providing a forum for your readers to give you feedback on the newsletter, you give them a chance to gain "ownership" of the newsletter. You should encourage ongoing communication with your readers and make them feel like partners in your organization.

✔ **18-9.** *Vary the contents.*

Too many newsletters provide only one type of article or feature. You need to explore many ways of presenting information to keep hooking your reader. If you use a lot of service pieces—how-to articles on relevant subjects—you might want to also include a letters column, which invites comments and ideas from readers.

Other possibilities include a Q&A column, which provides answers to readers' questions, guest articles by qualified specialists, and checklists of do's and don'ts to dramatize the contents of a service piece.

There's no end to topics you can cover in your newsletter, including:

Company news

Industry news

New products

Product improvements

New models

New accessories

New applications

Troubleshooting guides

Customer profiles

Quizzes

Contests

Announcements and write-ups of conferences, seminars, meetings, and trade shows

Community relations activities

Manufacturing success stories

Recent innovations in research and development

Case histories (product success stories)

✔ **18-10.** *Use article titles that promise the reader something.*

Traditionally, how-to articles are the foundation of newsletters. People want to learn how they can master their environment, and newsletters can fill them in. How-to articles stress not only how to do something but often what benefit will accrue. Hence, the book title *How to Win Friends and Influence People* not only promises how to do something but implies benefits of interest to almost everyone.

✔ **18-11.** *Use subheads to break up long chunks of type.*

Our eyes rebel against too much undifferentiated type. We need to be pulled back into lengthy articles by some type of unexpected graphic aid. Subheads fill the bill by catching our attention, telling us what the next few paragraphs are about, and, occasionally, highlighting a feature that will further motivate us to keep reading. For example, the article on "Conflict Can Be Positive" was broken up with headlines such as, "The ailment," "The remedy," "Success stories," "Tips for the HR manager," and "Three resolution skills." The article on choosing press kit photos was broken up with subheads such as "Finding a photographer," and "What it costs."

✔ **18-12.** *Vary your subheads.*

How-to headlines are only one of several types of possible headlines for stories in your newsletter. Other categories of headlines include the question headline, the command headline, the direct headline, and the reasons why headline.

The *question* headline pulls the reader into the headline (e.g., "Can You Survive the Recession?" or "Do You Need a Laser Printer?")

The *command* headline tells you to take action (e.g., "Make Sure You Vote on Tuesday," "Make the Most of Your Writing Talent," or "Recycle Your Old Newspapers and Help Save the Environment").

The *direct* headline has a news feeling to it and promises the reader something fresh and important (e.g., "An Ongoing Method of Saving Money" and "New Ways to Invest").

The *reasons why* headline is appropriate when you want to explain a topic quickly or distinguish an idea from others (e.g., "Two Reasons to Fund Your IRA," and "Four Reasons to Hire a Freelance Writer for Your Brochures").

✔ **18-13.** *Be original.*

A frequent mistake in distributing a newsletter is reiterating or encapsulating information published by other sources. Certainly, there are newsletters that can survive by recycling press releases, excerpts from executive speeches, and rehashed published articles and papers. After all, lengthy material that the reader might not normally finish can be condensed and rewritten to make it more readable. This can be marginally effective but fails to demonstrate your insider's understanding of the niche and the different and better aspects of your services. It is far better to use your newsletter to convey the results of your own research. Showcasing your own findings effectively conveys your deep understanding and separates you from the competition.

✔ **18-14.** *Identify your reader.*

Some businesses know just where to find their customer— by looking at the addresses on sales slips, by going to mailing lists, or by inventing methods such as guest books. If you can identify the people with whom you'd like to communicate, make a record of their names and addresses. You can either type each name on a master sheet (and then reproduce the names on pressure sensitive mailing labels) or, if you have a word processor, simply store the names, thus automating the process for repeat mailings.

If your newsletter is competing with others, it must have a distinctive angle. Ideally, a newsletter offers inside information, news that would be hard to find elsewhere. Or perhaps your method of distribution is unique or the frequency with which you publish.

The following are a few of the types of businesses that could profit from having a newsletter:

Management consultant

Bank

Publisher

Art gallery

Gift shop

Trade association

Business cooperative

Engineering firm

✔ **18-15.** *Tie your newsletter in with the calendar, if appropriate.*

For example, a party goods store in Stamford, Connecticut, puts out a newsletter that alerts its customers to seasonal party items and new ideas for celebrating holidays. It also offers creative ideas for planning successful parties. The blend of timeliness and specific, useful information never fails to bring about a surge in business soon after the letter has been distributed.

✔ **18-16.** *Articles should establish the who, what, and why in the first paragraph or two.*

Just as journalists who write news stories weave essential details into their first few sentences, you need to get to the point quickly, letting readers know what they're reading, why they're reading it, and what its value or importance is to them. The first paragraph of the article on choosing press photos, for example, establishes its purpose quickly:

> Many of our subscribers wanted information about how to select press kit photos that editors will want to run. We've put together this special section on photography to answer these questions....

✔ **18-17.** *Make the format, title, logo, and first page distinctive.*

People judge newsletters by their first page. So, you need to grab attention quickly. Your logo, if a clever blend of styling and typography, can help grab attention. So can the use of white space, which gives an open, uncluttered look. Halftones, reverses (e.g., white type against a black background) can also be eye catching, use of boldface subheads or boxed material can steer the reader to an important tip, idea, or reference.

Keep in mind when designing pages that readers "process" pages from right to left in a sideways U-pattern, often skipping the middle of a page, especially if the middle is broken by the fold or staple of a two-page spread.

Don't wait until the design stage to begin thinking about how to use graphic elements. Various surveys have shown that readers typically begin by looking at interesting photos, so be sure you use well-planned and well-executed photographs and illustrations on your pages.

Use photo captions as a way to communicate key points

in a story. Captions convey important information and shouldn't be treated as throw-aways.

✔ **18-18.** *Use pictures, bullets, boxes, checklists, and other ways of calling out information.*

To keep the reader visually stimulated, you need to break away from prose occasionally. You can use line drawings to illustrate an idea or present a quotation or other "called out" material in a special box or between ruled lines. The called out material calls attention to your text and acts as a type of caption for the whole article.

Bullet points are appropriate when you wish to communicate a list of parallel items, rules, ideas, or directions. Checklists can help the reader rivet attention on major ideas contained in an article (or suggested steps). Photos are appropriate when a picture will capture an image (e.g., what a tattoo looks like) better than words could possibly suggest.

✔ **18-19.** *Use experts to bolster article information.*

The newsletter should present a feeling of diversity to its audience. You can't be a sole source of information. When the newsletter for PR professionals, *PR Ink,* recently ran the story about what makes a good public relations photo, the last page of the newsletter was devoted to quotations from seven diverse media, including the Associated Press, *Baltimore Sun,* and *Sassy Magazine.* The quotations rounded off the ideas in the article and provided lively, first-hand anecdotes, opinions, and illustrations.

✔ **18-20.** *Keep your reader reading!*

Ask yourself, "What is the compelling reason to read my newsletter?" List the benefits of your newsletter, translating those benefits into practical actions that will be vital to your readers' lives. If you deal in coins, stamps, antiques, or fine art, a newsletter may provide a handy way of staying in touch with frequent customers. By telling them of trends, sales, and news events, you are reinforcing your image as an expert in the field and putting your name in front of customers on a regular basis.

PART 4

Technical Business Documents

19

Specifications

A *specification* (or spec) is a description of work to be done. You may write specifications for an air conditioner, a volleyball court, a lampshade, a milk container, or an airport ground control system. By writing a precise specification, you aid in the creation of a product that does what it's designed to do with maximum efficiency.

Since a specification is a formal statement of a customer's requirements, it helps to reveal dependencies, inconsistencies, ambiguities, and additional customer requirements while still in the early stages of development; this way, you avoid extensive and costly debugging and modification after the product is fully developed.

Here are some steps to follow when writing specs:

✔ **19-1.** *Get a statement of the problem and requirements from the customer.*

In the systems environment, this is called the *systems requirements specification*. If you are writing this kind of spec, be sure to state the problem and define the specific system needs. For example, for an automated teller machine (ATM), your customer, the XYZ Bank, has this problem statement: "Our bank needs a way to provide our clients with most banking services 24 hours a day. We have decided that an automated teller machine will meet those needs, and we need software to run it."

✔ **19-2.** *Analyze and classify the problem and requirements.*

Decide on the minimal set of basic functions, and try to specify them first. Basic functions for the ATM could be deposits, withdrawals, and transfers. From the customer's statement, you find that one requirement is to provide clients with most banking services 24 hours a day. Try to elaborate needs into statements of measurable results: "Human tellers take approximately two minutes to complete a routine transaction. The ATM should take no more than 45 seconds to complete routine transactions."

✔ **19-3.** *Restate this requirements specification in your words to the customer.*

By doing this, you get the customer to focus on the details of what is required before a spec is written.

✔ **19-4.** *Begin your design spec process.*

Once you've mapped out a systems requirements specification—in the systems environment, this tells what is required to meet the needs—you may write a design spec describing the process of *how* it is to be done. Now, here are some guidelines to help you avoid the common pitfalls in writing specifications.

✔ **19-5.** *Use clear technical language.*

Rather than avoiding technical language, assume that the customer has technical staff to review technical portions of the spec. Watch out for formal language, legalese, or punctuation that invites ambiguity, sounds stilted, or changes the meaning of the description.

✔ **19-6.** *Be precise and concise.*

State requirements as precisely as you understand and in a way that allows for testing once implemented. Use the fewest words to complete the description. Two or three short sentences are preferable to one long sentence.

Unclear   The updated data will be redisplayed within 5 seconds after the data are entered and validated.

Better   The updated data will be redisplayed within 5 seconds after the customer has entered data. The data will be validated by the system once it has been entered by the customer.

✔ **19-7.** *Be complete—but don't overdo it.*

Technical staffers sometimes think that to be "comprehensive" they must research and write about all the details or possibilities for a given requirement. But covering the important details doesn't imply covering everything. Concentrate initially on describing just the normal possibilities expected by the customer.

✔ **19-8.** *Use the present tense.*

Some specs use *should* or *must* or *will* when describing what the proposed system will do in the future. My preference is to keep specification descriptions in the present tense. For example:

The CPU is composed of six assemblies.

The CC monitors and controls the flow of signals.

The System Controller performs the following functions.

As in most writing, the present tense is dynamic and immediate. Once you start using it, you will be able to avoid the confusion of shifting from *should* to *will* to *is* to *must* that characterizes so many specifications.

20

Technical Manuals

Many large technological firms have departments that produce manuals about the company's products. Most software companies also use staff or outside technical writers to prepare manuals for their products. Systems development professionals are often responsible for creating the documentation that goes along with the systems they produce.

The following lists just a few of the many types of manuals technical writers are called upon to write. These may require separate volumes or may appear as sections of a single volume.

Installation manual: How to correctly and safely install a device or piece of equipment. Typically includes wiring diagrams and exploded views to aid in assembly.

Instruction manual: How to operate equipment. Usually shows control panels with call-outs indicating the function of each control or read out.

Sales manual: How to specify and purchase equipment. This manual contains product specifications, pricing, and other information salespeople use to sell products.

Effective manuals have the following characteristics:

☐ They are well written.

☐ They are attractively designed.

☐ Their format makes it easy for users to follow instructions accurately.

☐ They are illustrated appropriately to enhance understanding.

☐ They help people do their work correctly, efficiently, uniformly, and comfortably.

The following guidelines can help you write manuals that are easy to read and easy to follow.

✔ **20-1.** *Remember that manual writing is instruction writing.*

You will be a more effective writer of manuals if you keep in mind that your mission is to *give instruction*, not impress or dazzle your audience with your technical knowledge or prose style. Almost everyone dislikes reading manuals, so the easier you can make things for your reader, the better.

One way to improve your ability to write clear manuals is to practice giving instructions. If you have trouble giving clear directions to car drivers, for example, you'll probably have trouble explaining how to use CAD/CAM software or install a programmable controller.

Practice your ability to give clear instruction by writing instructions for nontechnical activities. For instance, you might try writing instructions on how to put on a necktie, then see if your 9-year-old son can follow them without help from you.

Writing workable instructions for seemingly simple acts is often quite difficult. But once you master this skill, you'll find writing instructions for technical activities is not much different—and not much more difficult.

✔ **20-2.** *Be complete.*

Give complete direction. It is better to assume too little knowledge, experience, and familiarity with your technology on the part of the reader than too much; I have never heard of any person complaining that a manual was too easy to follow.

Naturally, you must assume *some* knowledge on the part of the reader, but where do you draw the line? Visualize your target audience, and write for that audience so the *least experienced or skilled* member of that group can understand what you are saying and follow your directions.

Yet, there are some things—facts, terms, technical concepts, and so on—it is reasonable to assume your target audience knows. For example, it's reasonable to assume electricians understand the concepts of resistance and voltage or that they know how to splice wire, and so you need not explain these things in your manual.

When in doubt, it's a good idea to state explicitly in the preface or introduction of your manual who the intended audience is and what knowledge you assume on their part.

> This manual is intended to be used by technicians in installing the new Direct Residual Controller on existing chlorinator units. We assume the reader is familiar with chlorinator operations as well as the general principles of direct residual control.

> This manual assumes a basic grasp of computer programming and system design. No prior knowledge of object-oriented design is assumed or required.

✔ **20-3.** *Be clear and correct.*

You must strive to make manuals clear, direct, and easy to follow. Few things are as frustrating to the owner of a product than a manual he or she can't follow or one that contains errors—for example, an instruction sheet for a piece of furniture that says there are screw holes where there aren't any.

Even difficult procedures can be made clear through careful writing. In his book *How to Dissect: Exploring with Probe and Scalpel* (New York: Sentinel, 1961, p. 105), William Berman approaches the complex operation of dissecting a frog in a simple style. He doesn't make the instructions needlessly complicated simply because the subject is technical.

> The heart is encased in a sac called the *pericardial sac.* Cut through the thin membrane of this sac with the tip of a very sharp razor. Do not cut the heart itself. Then spread the membrane with forceps to expose the heart.

Although the procedure is complex, the language is plain, conversational, and human: Reading this manual is like having a patient tutor at your side, helping you step-by-step to perform the operation described. And that's how all good instruction manuals should be written.

✔ **20-4.** *Be unambiguous.*

Ambiguity in instructional materials makes readers uncomfortable and nervous. They want to be *sure* they're doing things right. If you feel your reader has the potential to be confused or uncertain about a particular task or procedure, repeating your instruction two or three times in different ways can help eliminate uncertainty and give the reader confidence.

A good manual is not only written so that it can be easily understood; ideally, it should be written so the instructions cannot be *mis*understood. And that's sometimes a tall order to fill.

William Berman, in his dissection instructions, says "Cut through the thin membrane of [the pericardial] sac with the tip of a very sharp razor." Although his instructions are *cut the membrane,* he wants to write so that he cannot be misunderstood, and adds, "Do not cut the heart itself."

While this may seem redundant—after all, if you're following step-by-step directions, and the directions don't instruct you to cut the heart, you wouldn't do it—but the author knows that cutting the heart is a common mistake students make, and so he emphasizes this point to be completely unambiguous.

✔ **20-5.** *Use warnings.*

Instruction writers are responsible for telling their readers what to do but must also take responsibility for telling their readers what *not* to do. If performing a certain task might accidentally erase a hard disk file, give the operator an electric shock, expose workers to toxic fumes, shut down the production line, or damage the equipment, you must explicitly warn the reader against doing that action.

Highlight warnings by setting them in boldface type, all capital letters, a large type face, or with other graphic technique. We feel putting a box around the warning is a good way to draw attention to it, because people always read text in boxes. Therefore, you can simply insert the warning into your document at the appropriate place, then make it stand out from the rest of the copy by drawing a box around it:

> **WARNING:** BL-2000 filter is designed for industrial and municipal use only and should not be used in swimming pools, parks, or for other recreational purposes.

Boxed warnings should be used sparingly and reserved for only the most important warnings. Overusing boxes or any other graphic technique makes it less effective. (For example, underlining a word on a page draws attention to it. But if you underline every other word, then no word stands out.)

Secondary warnings—those instructions you want to emphasize because of their importance but feel do not warrant the box treatment—can be put in italics, underlined, or emphasized using some other graphic convention. You can also reinforce the importance of a warning or instruction by preceding it with the words *make sure*, as in these examples:

Before applying power, make sure the power supply in the equipment conforms to the form of primary power available.

Before closing the panel, make sure the screws are tight.

Make sure the set point does not exceed safe levels.

✔ **20-6.** *Use the imperative voice.*

Instruction manuals are written in the imperative mode.

Be direct. It's better to write *connect the communications line* than the weaker, more passive *the communications line should be connected*. As shown in the example below, effective instructions tell the reader what to do in the simplest, most direct language possible.

Connect one end of the line cord with J3 on the back panel. This cord includes a ground wire for plugging into a grounded outlet. Before applying power, make sure the power supply in the equipment conforms to the form of primary power available. Required fuses are listed below.

When writing in the imperative mode, you begin sentences with an action verb instructing the reader to perform a certain task. These action verbs include:

attach	connect	examine
begin	detach	expose
check	determine	find
close	disconnect	finish

fix	make sure	repair
grasp	measure	restore
hold	monitor	screw
increase	open	select
install	place	take
join	prepare	test
let	provide	tighten
loosen	push	type
lubricate	put	unpack
make	remove	verify

✔ **20-7.** *Choose an organizational scheme appropriate to the task, the audience, and the technology.*

One of the first steps in writing a manual is to decide how you will organize your material.

The organizational scheme can be presented either as an outline or in a descriptive memo explaining how you intend to organize your document (and why).

This written "proposal" for your organizational scheme should be reviewed and approved by management *before* you begin writing. Although technical errors and poor style are relatively easy to correct at any stage, changing the organizational scheme after a draft has been written is an expensive and time-consuming task. Therefore, an organizational structure should be selected and agreed upon before the writing begins.

The two basic organizational schemes used by instruction writers are *sequential organization* and *functional organization.*

In sequential organization, you organize your material according to the steps your reader must take to complete a task or master a subject matter. Using sequential organization in a manual for a word processing software package, for example, you might start with a few "quick and dirty" instructions so the user can immediately begin using the program to write simple memos and letters. Then you can get into more sophisticated word processing, such as footnotes, underlining, boldfacing, page formatting, and page numbering. The benefit of sequential organization is that it allows the reader to achieve quick results, without a lot of reading, and it also helps the reader master the skill faster—because it's designed to fit how the reader thinks about the subject.

The disadvantage of sequential organization? Because the manual is designed for learning, it's an excellent tool for training novices but not such a good tool for the experienced user who is more interested in reference than instruction. Also, by being task-oriented rather than function- or feature-oriented, the sequential manual may have a lot of repetition and cross-referencing; for example, the same instruction sequence may be repeated half a dozen times or more as it applies to different tasks or operations.

Functional organization means the manual is organized around the functions or features of the system or equipment being described. A functionally organized manual for a word processing package, for example, might have separate chapters on page formatting, text processing, text moving and manipulation, on-screen graphics, printing documents, saving documents as files, exporting files to other programs, and so on.

The functional organization scheme has two advantages. First, because it's organized around the way the product is designed, it's easier to outline and write. You just follow the product features or functions. With a sequential manual, which is organized based on what the reader wants to know and do rather than on what the product functions are, you have to spend a lot more time thinking about, "Well, what exactly do the readers want to learn, and what's the best way to teach it to them?"

A second advantage of functional manuals is that they are better organized for reference use. Once you know how to use the system, you may prefer a functional manual because it's easy to look up and find the description of the specific function or feature you want to activate.

The disadvantage of functional manuals is that they are not ideal learning tools because they do not present a step-by-step process for achieving specific results.

You select the organizational scheme based on usage. A manual for a training course would probably be sequential, whereas a reference manual for use after training might be functional. Many manufacturers produce one of each type of manual or combine them in a single document.

Strive to make your organizational scheme obvious and transparent to the reader, rather than subdued or subtle. The more apparent the organizational scheme, the easier your document is to follow.

One way to support the organizational scheme is through the use of "guideposts"—a table of contents, introduction, headings, page breaks, index, tabs, and any other devices you can think of to guide the reader through your document.

✔ **20-8.** *Present instructions as a series of numbered steps.*

If an operation is clearly a step-by-step procedure, you can make life easier for the reader by writing the instruction manual as a series of numbered steps.

START-UP OPERATION FOR POLYMER MIXER

1. With the injection unit fully retracted, bring the barrel and mixer to operating temperature.
2. Wet the machine operation mode to manual and the boost and secondary pressure regulators to their lowest settings.
3. Quickly depress and release the injection switch. If the screw bounces back, allow more heat soaking time.
4. Once the polymer flows freely in a purging mode,

increase the injection pressure as required and begin the molding operation.

With numbered steps, if the operator needs to discuss the procedure with your support staff, they can ask a question by referring to "step 3" instead of "the fifth line down in the second paragraph on the fourth page, where it says to release the whatchamacallit switch."

✔ **20-9.** *Use a modular approach.*

In a modular approach, sections are numbered in outline form using a hierarchical system. A heading that reads

3.4.2 Unplugging the spray head

means this material appears in subsection 2 of section 4 in Chapter 3. The advantage of this modular scheme is that it makes it easy to delete, replace, insert, and expand sections to make corrections or update the manual to be current as new releases or versions of the system are introduced.

For example, if the new model has an automatic water-jet that washes down the spray head to prevent accumulation of solids that can plug the head, you can add a section as follows:

3.4.2.1 Operation of spray head self-cleaning water-jet feature

This can be inserted as a new sub-subsection immediately following the existing text of subsection 3.4.2 on unplugging the spray head.

✔ **20-10.** *Test drive your manual.*

Although engineers, programmers, and system designers will review manuals for accuracy, the true test of a manual's effectiveness is whether a typical user can follow it. For this reason, we recommend that you "test drive" your manuals before you have them duplicated in quantity. This is accomplished by making a few photocopies of the preliminary draft, giving them to a few typical users, and getting their reaction.

Time, money, and deadlines limit the extent to which you can pretest the manual. At some point, you have to create your final draft and get it published. Most manufacturers, however, err on the side of doing too little rather than too much testing of manuals.

21

Technical Reports

Technical reports may be difficult to write, but they are vitally important. Why? Because they are the showcases of your work and should demonstrate your effectiveness.

Technical reports are the documents in which engineers, scientists, and managers transmit the results of their research, field work, and other activities to people in their organization. Often a written report is the only tangible product of hundreds of hours of work. Rightly or wrongly, the quality and worth of that work are judged by the quality of the written report—its clarity, organization, and content. Therefore, it pays to take the time to write a good report.

Here are a few tips that can help:

✔ **21-1.** *Know the sections of technical reports.*

Although research reports can take many forms, most contain the following major sections: cover, title page, abstract, table of contents, summary, body, results, conclusions, and recommendations. There may also be a section on nomenclature, references, and an appendix.

✔ **21-2.** *Keep the cover page simple.*

The cover and title page create the reader's first impression of your report. The cover should be cleanly typed but not gaudy—no border, stars, or similar treatments. The title page should be neat; the title should tell the reader exactly what the report is about.

✔ **21-3.** *Provide an abstract and table of contents for lengthy reports.*

The abstract is an informative, concise, one-paragraph statement of the work performed, its objectives and scope, and the major conclusions reached. The table of contents can help the reader grasp the sections of a lengthy report, since the contents lists every section heading and subheading and the page numbers on which they appear. Tables, figures, charts, and graphs are listed separately at the end.

✔ **21-4.** *Summarize your report.*

Whereas the abstract gives the reader enough information to decide whether to read the report, the summary presents its entire contents in a few hundred words—usually one page or less. It covers the purpose of the work, the goal, the scientific or commercial objective, what was done, how it was done, and the key results. Summaries are usually not included in reports of fewer than 25 pages.

✔ **21-5.** *Give your purpose for writing the report in the introduction.*

The introduction tells readers—including those not familiar with the subject matter or the reason for writing the report—the purpose of the report. It provides background material, theory, and explanation of why the work was done and what it accomplished.

✔ **21-6.** *Use the introduction to set the scene for your report.*

A helpful introduction does many things, including

- Presenting the nature and scope of the investigated problem
- Putting into perspective the importance of the research as it relates to scientific knowledge or commercial operations
- Discussing findings from previous research
- Stating the method of investigation
- Presenting the key results of the research

✔ 21-7. *Separate the theory behind the work from the results.*

Put in the *body* of the report the detailed theory behind the work. Also, outline the apparatus and procedures used so that other researchers can follow these steps and repeat the experiment.

In the *results* section, present experimental data, observations, and results, along with a discussion of the meaning, significance, importance, and application of these results. Point out any exceptions or lack of correlation; explain (if possible) why such exceptions or deviations occurred; show how the results compare with results achieved by other researchers.

✔ 21-8. *Give conclusions and recommendations based on your evidence.*

The conclusions are a series of numbered statements showing how the results answered questions raised in the stated purpose of the research. On the basis of the results and conclusions, the researcher can make recommendations about whether further research is needed or how the results can be applied commercially.

22

User Manuals

Poorly written manuals have plagued computer users for decades—probably since the first electronic computer, Eniac, was switched on in 1946. A clear, easy-to-follow manual can increase productivity, save money, speed acceptance, and increase usage of a new software product or computer system. Here are 10 guidelines for your manual writers to live by. These tenets will ensure that your organization's manuals communicate the right message to users.

✔ 22-1. *Organize logically.*

The best way to organize most computer manuals is by user tasks rather than by machine functions. The distinction makes a world of difference to users. They're much more concerned about how the product can help them on their jobs than about how the system works.

To ensure that manuals are sensibly organized, direct your writers to first make an outline. They can use the items in the outline as headings and subheadings in the final version. This procedure will help writers prepare manuals that reflect your organization's organizational scheme and will break the text into short, easy-to-read sections.

✔ 22-2. *Use numbered step-by-step instructions.*

Clear instructions leave no room for doubt. Use the active narrative voice: Start sentences with imperatives and use direct statements. For example, the manual accompanying a database package guides the reader with instructions:

Step 1. Type "UNISTOX."

Step 2. Type the report numbers you have located in Source Digest or Data Reports.

When your writers start instructions with the imperative form of a verb, the reader instantly knows what to do. Imperatives cut unnecessary verbiage too.

✔ 22-3. *Minimize cross-references.*

The overuse of cross-references makes manuals hard to follow. Here's a real-life example:

In order for the FOCUS Report Writer (see Section 2.3.1) to read a TOTAL Database (see Database manual), the user or project designer must prepare a FOCUS Data Description (see Section 3.4.1.1) that is equivalent to the TOTAL Database structure (see Appendix C).

Instead of learning the system, the user will spend most of his or her time frantically turning pages, switching from section to section for instructions or descriptions vital to understanding what she or he is reading.

Cross-references are frustrating and confusing. Use only cross-references that are absolutely necessary for the user to understand the material.

✔ 22-4. *Repeat procedures until the user gets them right.*

For example, the user has to go through the logging-on procedure regardless of which function he or she wants to perform. Should the manual repeat the procedure under every section or assume the user got it right the first time?

We recommend repeating basic procedures (loading disks, accessing programs, using menus) until you can be reasonably certain that the user is comfortable with them. When the manual writer reaches that point with the users, procedures can be reduced to simple statements such as "log onto the system" or "set margins for standard paper."

✔ **22-5.** *Show users—don't tell them.*

Employees would rather *do* than *read.* Keep descriptive text to a minimum; most of the manual should give the user instructions to follow at a terminal or personal computer.

✔ **22-6.** *Use lots of illustrations.*

When words cannot adequately describe a thought, the manual writer should use illustrations. For example, in addition to writing "put the tape reel on the take-up drive," present a picture of how the tape reel fits onto the drive.

✔ **22-7.** *White space and the right typeface make the manual easier to read.*

Readers appreciate the clear, uncluttered look of a manual that uses wide margins and lots of blank, or "white," space.

If the manual will not change, typeset the text to give it a clean professional look. Typeset text makes manuals more legible, and it also introduces an element of familiarity. It will help manuals seem like real books, as opposed to slapdash imitations of books.

If your manual will be updated frequently, you'll probably want to reproduce typed pages or printer output to save money. Three-ring binders are usually best for manuals that are revised frequently. If a section or a page is changed, you can distribute just the changed portion, not a revision of the whole manual.

✔ **22-8.** *Add guideposts to add readability.*

Another ploy to keep the reader on track is adding guideposts—a table of contents, introduction, index, and tabs. The table of contents outlines all sections and subsections of the manual. The index should cover key terms and concepts but not every word in the manual. If a user wonders what to do when a disk is filled to capacity, he or she should be able to find the entry, "Disk, full" in the index.

✔ **22-9.** *Break the tension.*

Although the manual should be written in a straightforward instructional tone, an occasional pun, joke, or other human interruption can break the tension and help put nervous computer novices at ease. Here's an example from one of the many guides that's been written for the IBM Personal Computer—*The IBM PC Guide* by James Kelley (Banbury Books, $30):

> We need just 10 of the 2155 characters in IBM's extended set. Thus, we ought to be able to pack some 25.5 times more numeric information into a byte than is permitted by the ASCII coding scheme. That seems reasonable, doesn't it?
>
> In fact, this is exactly what is done in practice. I'm not going to put a glaze in your eyes by explaining the arcane coding schemes used—I'd have to look them up anyway!

✔ **22-10.** *Test drive your manual.*

Although your technical communications pros will probably review a manual writer's work, the true test of a manual's effectiveness is that it is so easy that "any old user" can understand it. So, give drafts of manuals to a few typical users for a tryout.

For instance, if a manual helps bank tellers access checking-account balances, give them the manual and see if they can follow the instructions. If they have trouble, so will your organization. Better send your manual writer back to the drawing board. If the users can follow the instructions, you can be confident the manual—and the new automated tool—will be successful.

23

ISO 9000
Quality Policy Manuals

ISO 9000 is a quality standard that is sweeping the world. Many manufacturers find themselves pressured to obtain ISO 9000 certification to please their customers. Others find that ISO certification is a worthy goal because it helps them hone their quality systems. In any case, ISO 9000 requires documentation—quality policy manuals, procedures, and work instructions—that is clear, concise, and specific.

The *quality policy manual* is management's statement of policy toward ensuring quality products and a systematic approach to maintaining quality standards. These manuals are written to conform to the ISO 9000 standards and are usually modeled on those standards. For example, a company trying to get certified for ISO 9001 must write a manual that encompasses 20 separate areas of concern—everything from the establishment of a quality system to methods for handling defects to the establishment of training to ensure qualified personnel.

Here are some tips on writing quality policy manuals for the ISO 9000 standards:

✔ **23-1.** *While preparing to meet ISO 9000 standards, write an action plan listing every activity that must be accomplished along the way.*

Before starting to pursue ISO 9001, the quality manager at Symbol Technologies wrote an action plan of 267 steps—that was just for creating the quality manual. The plan listed every task, the people responsible for it, and an estimated time to complete.

The first task, "List all procedures that are associated with each clause," was estimated to take a week.

This type of global thinking is also exemplified by the quality manager at Dynepco, who sent out a long memo to his staff about achieving certification for ISO 9002. The memo, part strategy and part pep talk, listed 16 steps toward achieving certification. The first four are:

1. Obtain management commitment.

2. Appoint a management representative to lead the process.

3. Form a steering committee or team that includes hourly people and has all areas represented.

4. Educate the team about the ISO registration process.

✔ **23-2.** *Keep your ISO 9000 quality policy manual to fewer than 40 pages.*

The quality policy manual is sometimes thought of as pointing to or referencing lower-level documents. The quality manual is not the place to go into detail about who does what or how things are done. It is a place to set policy.

The quality manual should contain no proprietary material. In fact, it should be written as if it were to be given to customers, and, in some cases, competitors. If the manual is running longer than 40 pages, you are probably going into more depth than necessary or are being redundant. At that point, your manual will start to resemble a list of procedures or work instructions.

✔ **23-3.** *Model your quality manual after the ISO 9000 standards.*

The order of the topics in the ISO standard should guide you in the organization of your quality policy manual. Even if you have a manual partially written, it's best to start again, mirroring the topics and order of the particular ISO 9000 standard in which your company is trying to become certified. By making the manual's topics the same as ISO's, you are helping potential auditors follow your thoughts and make sure you've covered the required topics.

✔ **23-4.** *Make quality manuals easily auditable and maintainable.*

Making a quality manual auditable means making it easy to read, easy to reference, and easy to reread. By reflecting the ISO 9000 standards, the manual becomes easier to audit quickly.

Other format issues to consider include wide margins (lots of white space makes reading easy on the eyes); consistent spacing (helps highlight what's important); consistent numbering (shows readers which topics are subsets of others); large serif typefaces (help readability: save italics for emphasis only); correct capitalization; and title blocks that have the name of the company, document name, revision or signature line, page number, and document number.

Title blocks help you maintain your manual by making it easy to see where revised pages fit and by telling you the last time a document has been revised.

✔ **23-5.** *When trying to explain your tasks to a layperson, ask yourself, "How would I explain this to a very bright child?"*

When talking to children, you automatically know to boil down difficult-to-grasp concepts. The same idea should apply when circulating documents to people who are not versed in your technical field. Don't expect that they "know it." They may not. They often need help from you in forming a mental image of the product or process you are trying to describe.

Avoid vague phrases such as "To ensure that the requirements between ACME Company and its customers are effectively communicated...." *Which* requirements? Contractual? Procedures? Don't make the reader guess. "Use the correct word and not," as Mark Twain once said, "its second cousin."

24

ISO 9000 Procedures

ISO 9000 is a quality standard that is sweeping the world. Many manufacturers find themselves pressured to obtain ISO 9000 certification to please their customers. Others find that ISO certification is a worthy goal because it helps them hone their quality systems. In any case, ISO 9000 requires documentation—quality manuals, procedures, and work instructions—that is clear, concise, and specific.

Here are some tips on writing procedures for the ISO 9000 standards:

✔ **24-1.** *Write ISO 9000 procedures that are specific but do not handcuff your people in completing their work.*

If you were writing, for example, a procedure on how a report was to be bound, you might write:

> Put all sheets in a Clear-Vue see-through report cover and thread a black spine over the left side of the cover to bind the report.

But what if you run out of Clear-Vue covers? Are others just as good? And what about those black spines? Would a green one make a big difference? Perhaps you could write:

Put all sheets in a see-through report cover and thread a spine over the left side of the cover to bind the report.

✔ **24-2.** *If any of those who must write ISO 9000 procedures are inexperienced writers, have them create flowcharts describing their tasks.*

While flowcharts are not a substitute for narrative in an ISO procedure, they can help procedure writers explain what they do. Many engineers think visually, and it's easier for them to do a flowchart than to construct a paragraph or even a series of bullet points.

Flowcharts should be easy to read and contain fewer than eight steps. Try to fashion a set of procedures based on the flowchart.

Streamline procedures by bulleting procedures' parallel items, especially those that start with verbs. Often, there's no need to put procedures in paragraph form. For example, instead of a paragraph filled with items separated by commas or semicolons, break out of the paragraph using a colon and bullet points to line up the thoughts for the reader.

✔ **24-3.** *Keep procedures concise.*

Don't throw in the kitchen sink. Like every other type of writing, documentation is selective and should contain the minimum amount necessary to convey the idea.

Avoid redundancies like, "All quality systems, current and new, used by...." Knock out "current and new." Here's another redundancy: "The Sales Division will completely document all the processes that affect the customer/supplier relationship between Acme and its customers." Leave out "customer/supplier."

Avoid wordy expressions (e.g., "on an annual basis") and the obvious (e.g., "All staff reporting directly or indirectly will support this policy.")

Avoid clichés and puffery such as "quality is the basis of our corporate culture" or "we will produce perfect products and services every time on time."

✔ **24-4.** *Make procedures self-explanatory and authoritative.*

Emerson once said you should write not just so that you'll be understood but so that you cannot be misunderstood. To do this, you need to delete any hedging. Get rid of words like *basically, perhaps, under certain circumstances,* and *in most cases.*

Here's a vague and weak purpose statement: "To assign the responsibilities and authorities of the various departments within the company." Here's a sharper, more authoritative version: "To ensure individual department compliance with quality management system guidelines for managing responsibilities."

✔ **24-5.** *Use hierarchical, easy-to-follow numbering systems for sections and subsections.*

Stay consistent:

1.0 PURPOSE
2.0 SCOPE
3.0 DEFINITIONS

The headings are all capitals. Subtopics are indented and are lined up underneath the heading:

3.0 DEFINITIONS

    3.1 Document—the original media that conveys information or proof of an activity, task, or procedure.
    3.2 Standard Operating Procedure
    3.3 Process Sheet

✔ **24-6.** *Tell what* not *to do when personal safety or other danger is involved.*

Although procedures usually give instructions to follow, some procedures specifically tell what not to do when danger may be involved. A procedure for mixing chemicals, handling medical waste, or cleaning up an oil spill may instruct a person *not* to use bare hands when holding a used needle or *not* to mix certain chemicals without wearing protective goggles.

✔ **24-7.** *Those actually using procedures should, at least, review them and, preferably, have a large role in writing them.*

No one knows how to do a particular job better than the person who does it every day. And, even though that person may not be a skilled writer, he or she should at least have a say in how the procedure is written. This input helps make the procedure more realistic and more accurate. If possible, the same person who does the task should write the procedure.

✔ **24-8.** *Use the imperative voice.*

By using the imperative voice you add a ring of authority to a procedure. Start each step of a procedure with a verb that directs the reader. Starting with verbs keeps you in the active voice and tells the reader *who* does *what*. It's better to write "shake the solution gently" than "the solution should be shaken gently." With the latter, there's a bit of fuzziness—*who*, exactly, does the shaking?

PART 5

Other Business Documents

25

Business Plans

You may wonder why you should write a business plan for yourself. After all, you know your own business, so there is no need to write things down. It would be like talking to yourself.

That is just what you should do: Get in touch with the nature of your business and with its goals. Do it for yourself and for any stranger, customer, or investor who may be less familiar with the nature of what you do and why you do it.

A great drama critic once said that writing a review helped him discover his true feelings about a play he had just seen. Sometimes, in the act of writing the review, initial impressions were clarified and refined. Sometimes the adrenalin and excitement generated by the curtain calls mask the hollowness of the play itself. This holds true for a business idea. If it has merit, that merit can only be enhanced by describing it—in writing—in measurable, observable terms. Here are a few tips to help you hone your own business plan:

✔ **25-1.** *Summarize your business succinctly.*

Describe the nature of your business and its goals in a single sentence. It's a great exercise in focus and discipline. Here are some examples:

Lucullus is a deluxe restaurant in the grand European tradition, serving international cuisine and devoted to the serious diner.

Millimeter is a trade magazine providing information to technical professionals in the film and videotape field.

Bon-Bon is a travel agency specializing in meeting the needs of show business professionals who travel with a large personal staff.

✔ **25-2.** *State your objectives.*

The second part of your written plan is a statement of objectives. What would you like your business to become? What would you like to get out of it? Where do you want it to be in a year? In five years? Here are some statements of objectives:

My objectives are (1) to create advertising copy for leading industries along the Eastern seaboard, (2) to work at home, (3) to retire at age 55, and (4) to spend two months each year writing books.

Lucullus aims at (1) gaining an international reputation for excellent cuisine, (2) being booked for two weeks in advance, (3) being an "in" spot for celebrities and power brokers, and (4) maintaining excellent standards of food preparation, service, and presentation.

After coming up with objectives, you may want to communicate them to your lawyer, your accountant, and others who will figure prominently in your business. I urge you to do this as a way of furthering communication among your employees and helping to make the objectives more realistic.

✔ **25-3.** *Discuss trends that may affect your business's growth.*

Try to predict the future by studying and then writing about trends that will have a strong, positive impact on your business. This is not crystal-ball gazing; it is your best thinking about societal trends that may shape what you do in the coming years. Here are samples of how three businesses discussed trends within their business plans:

> The Communication Workshop recognizes the boom in interest in ISO 9000, a quality standard that is sweeping the world and that requires lots of written documentation. Since thousands of companies will be pressured into being certified in ISO 9000, they will need to write quality manuals, procedures, and work instructions. Many of these will be written by technical people with an aversion to writing. The Communication Workshop will offer public and on-site seminars in "Writing for ISO 9000" to meet this growing market.

> *Millimeter Magazine*, although once focused on technical people in the fields of film and videotape, sees rich new markets in the growing cable industry and in music video in particular. Perhaps, in the future, more of our editorial content and covers should focus on people in the forefront of the cable revolution.

> Rob's Ribs caters to the current popularity of Tex-Mex cuisine and plans to capitalize on this trend by offering ribs on a take-out basis and by introducing Texas-style barbecue to the North Shore of Long Island.

✔ **25-4.** *Take inventory of your resources.*

This means listing your assets, both those that show up on a balance sheet and those that do not. Do you have sufficient money, equipment, and space to realize your goals? If not, do you have a realistic expansion program and the ability to raise needed capital? Can you assemble a staff with the appropriate skills and education to help you accomplish your business objectives?

✔ **25-5.** *Ask yourself the hard questions during your inventory.*

Honest answers to the following questions can help you evaluate your resources and assets:

1. How much money do I have on hand? How long can I last if I hit a dry spell?

2. Do I, as the head of a business, have the skills and knowledge needed to make the business a success? If not, how can I acquire this expertise? What schooling, courses, seminars, books, cassettes, or networking techniques would help me?

3. How many key employees do I plan to have? Will I be able to find backup people who are trained and experienced enough to step in when I need extra help?

✔ **25-6.** *Set up intermediate goals and a timetable for meeting them.*

For example, if one of your business goals is to gross $1 million in sales, this step will map out precisely how you plan to accomplish it. How many items would you have to sell at a particular price? How many projects would you need to take on during a calendar year? At what fee?

✔ **25-7.** *Plan the steps needed to meet your marketing goals.*

If your goal is to send a letter to all your prospects four times a year or to generate five new clients annually by using direct mail, you might plan these steps: (1) shop for a computer and printer, (2) earmark a percentage of your income to buy the computer and the printer, (3) investigate ways of getting trained on the computer, (4) purchase appropriate mailing lists of prospective clients, (5) buy the computer and printer, (6) input the mailing list and create copy for the direct mail piece, (7) buy a supply of envelopes and letterhead, (8) send out the mailings, and (9) monitor the response to determine precisely your return on investment.

✔ **25-8.** *Show potential investors evidence of customer acceptance.*

You should indicate that the product or service is being used in the marketplace. You might begin with a broad look at the market you serve. How big is it? How will your idea fit in? What share of the market can you hope to obtain? If, for example, your dream is to open a chain of fast-food Indian restaurants, you should try to show that there is a vast market for fast food and that people are growing weary of take-out Italian, Chinese, barbecue, and burger restaurants.

✔ **25-9.** *Show an appreciation of an investor's needs.*

Provide evidence that investors will be able to cash in their stock in three to seven years after making their investment. If you are showing your business plan to a bank or to venture capitalists, it will be wise to have a detailed list of start-up and operating expenses projected for the first three years. You should also indicate a breakeven point.

✔ **25-10.** *Show evidence of managerial focus.*

Concentrate your efforts on what you do best. Investors want to make sure that the best possible management team is running the show. So, your business plan should show off your credentials and apply them to the type of business you are planning.

✔ **25-11.** *Demonstrate a proprietary position in the field.*

Try to obtain exclusive rights to a product or process. This can be in the form of a patent, copyright, or trademark. You might include evidence of these proprietary materials in your plan when you present it to investors.

26

Proposal Writing

These tips will help you write a winning proposal:

✔ **26-1.** *Learn everything you can about your client or the people who will evaluate your proposal.*

You have access to a lot of information—your prospective client's annual reports, company periodicals, advertisements and publicity, and previous requests for proposals (RFPs). Some RFPs include a "point of contact," usually someone who is involved in drafting the RFP and who can answer technical questions about the form and content of your proposal. Call that person. You can never tell when, in a seemingly innocuous conversation about a technical matter, the point of contact may reveal some information that can give you a competitive edge or at least a more customized approach to solving the prospect's problem.

One proposal evaluator we know has a checklist of items he looks for in each proposal that crosses his desk. If he were to receive a request for that checklist from a person about to submit a proposal to him, he'd send it. In other words, his criteria for evaluating proposals are there for the asking and *not proprietary*. Yet to date, no proposal writers have called him with questions, so they don't even know the checklist exists! The moral: Ask questions.

✔ **26-2.** *Sell your ideas by fitting them into your reader's needs.*

It's a mistake to launch into a discussion about your credentials or *your* approach without first stating the reader's or prospective client's needs. Prospective clients want to make sure you understand what they need before you start proposing a way to meet that need. If a reader needs to save money, you must slant all your ideas toward the goal of achieving cost effectiveness.

Suppose the client's project suggests that its overall agenda is, for example, to achieve independence by creating an in-house training staff to run its corporate training courses; then your proposal should reinforce your desire to help the client achieve independence. In fact, independence should be the overarching vision or theme that coalesces all facets of the proposed project.

In a proposal to create a scheduling system for another airline, the writer focused on the 10 years his department had spent developing such a system internally. Although the amount of time is worth mentioning, that fact should have been woven into a sentence highlighting how the department's experience could benefit the client. So, instead of writing "We have spent 10 years developing a new scheduling system for our company," the proposer should have written, "Our 10 years' experience developing our own scheduling system means lower development costs and faster start-up time for you."

✔ **26-3.** *Write an executive summary that will be understood by all levels of proposal readers.*

Proposals are evaluated by a wide variety of readers, from top management to technical evaluators to budget analyzers. These readers will focus on different sections of a proposal, perhaps skipping whole segments. All readers, however, should be able to evaluate the first section of a proposal, which is a summary of the document.

Although the name *executive summary* is helpful for discussion purposes, it doesn't have to be called that in your proposal. In fact, it is much more helpful to call it something that emphasizes a sales approach. Some examples: *Summary of Leading Features, Summary of Benefits, What XYZ Company Proposes to Do for You.*

The length of an executive summary can vary greatly. In an informal report, you may have just a paragraph; in a more formal report, the summary may be one page; and in a very formal report, the summary may be several pages.

✔ **26-4.** *Recognize the critical factors that evaluators use in assessing proposals.*

All elements in an RFP are not of equal importance to the client. Some RFPs actually weight each section, telling the reader which factors are of greater importance in deciding to whom to award the contract.

Some critical factors used by evaluators that can be turned to your advantage are: the length of time you have been in business; the date by which you say you can complete the project; project design; review of alternatives; travel expenses; reliability; or experience in completing similar work for other clients.

You should consider emphasizing other strengths as well. These may include:

1. Management reputation

2. Qualifications of key people

3. Reputation as an innovator

4. Modernization of facilities

5. Size of facilities

6. Reputation for lack of cost overruns

Just don't get carried away and overstate your assets or promise more than you can deliver.

✔ **26-5.** *Make sure your proposal addresses every element in an RFP.*

This is a difficult lesson to learn. Often, people responding to an RFP have "selective perception" (i.e., address only those issues in the RFP in which they are well versed). But clients may want you to speak to every point, even seemingly insignificant ones. If an RFP specifies that you prepare an hour-by-hour schedule of a course you propose to teach, don't try to "get by" with an overview of the class. Do exactly what the RFP asks you to do, even if it seems unnecessary (e.g., making a breakdown of anticipated expenses, even if you think the expenses will be minimal). If there's anything in the RFP or criteria that isn't clear or that you don't understand, ask for an explanation.

✔ **26-6.** *Separate fact from opinion.*

The worst thing you can do is to offer value judgments with which the client can disagree. You want to seem sober, fair, objective, and factual. Only after you build a foundation of fact can you offer a few judgments (e.g., "an on-site seminar is expensive and, therefore, not an alternative to a video program in stress management"); otherwise, you are likely to invite the reader to prove you wrong. The facts are your findings and should be labeled as such; opinions are conclusions and should be labeled that way. The following phrases, presented as facts in various proposals, are in reality opinions of the proposal writers:

> We are the recognized world leader in Yield Management System design. (Name clients or use quotes to make factual.)

> The Power 5 workstation offers powerful graphics capabilities. (Describe the graphics and let reader decide they are "powerful.")

Since 1983, our company has directed significant investments toward creating cost-effective microcircuits. (Include details on the investment so reader may conclude they are "significant.")

We offer a wide range of expertise. (List the areas you cover and let the reader decide that your expertise covers a "wide range.")

✔ **26-7.** *Use appropriate graphics to highlight your ideas and make them easy to visualize.*

Attention-getting graphics can play a vital part in winning a proposal. People are influenced by the ease with which they read your proposal, and clear, crisp graphics can dramatize your ideas.

Boldfaced headings and subheads are attention-getting and can guide the reader into your paragraphs. Bullet points are appropriate for lists of parallel ideas (e.g., abilities of a piece of software). Margins, of course, should be liberal—about $1\frac{1}{4}$ inches on both sides—giving the reader lots of white space.

Use charts, graphs, and tables when the information will be better displayed in those layouts than in prose form. For example, one proposal we saw tried to describe a "three-tiered" approach to a problem, with each tier building on the one before. Each tier or stage was very complex in itself and would have been bolstered by a chart that helped readers differentiate among the three stages.

Graphics are also useful when you want to stress a point, when the reader's knowledge is limited, to show tabular relationships, and to illustrate definitions or explanations, adding clarity to your words. To use graphics effectively, you should:

1. Accurately label them. Include complete identification, including number, title, and caption.

2. Include complete dimensions. Specify units of measure or scale.

3. Spell out words whenever possible rather than using abbreviations. If abbreviations are used, include a key.

4. Include a complete textual reference. Don't assume that the reader will check the graphic unless you refer to it. Examples of textual references include "as illustrated in Figure 2" and "(see Table 3)."

5. Specify the focus or interpretation you want the reader to apply when examining the graphic. Without a sentence to identify the significance of the graphic, the reader may not understand its purpose. An example: "Table 5 shows the rapid increase of CRTs during a 5-year period."

✔ **26-8.** *Delete words, sentences, and phrases that do not add to your meaning.*

Adding more words to your proposal does not add importance—just dead weight. Don't puff up your language or pad out your ideas. Try to write the most concise proposal possible. But remember, brevity is not conciseness: You could have a 50-page concise proposal simply because there's that much to put into it. If you can express everything in a few pages, however, don't try to dress up a 5-page proposal until it weighs in at 25 pages.

✔ **26-9.** *Create—don't boilerplate.*

There's a tendency to rely on *boilerplate*—static, standard sentences, paragraphs, or pages that seem to fit all situations and, therefore, do not change from proposal to proposal. After all, it's easy for you just to let your word processor grind out something close to what was written for an earlier client, but don't do it. Clients think of themselves as unique, and the last thing you want is for a prospective client to believe that you are just "phoning in" the proposal, recycling old solutions. You must try to create the ideas to fit the particular client and try not to copy old ideas because you don't feel like originating specific new ones. If your solutions and ideas sound "off the shelf," vague, and sketchy, you will not succeed.

✔ **26-10.** *Choose specific and concrete terms over vague generalities.*

Vagueness will not be counted in your favor. If you must be vague about a date or a dollar amount, point out the source of the vagueness (e.g., airline fares are in flux, or you aren't sure what the French franc will be worth next year).

Generalities may be convenient to use and come easily to mind, but they force the reader to work to figure out your exact meaning. Instead of writing, "This will give us enough time to reach some meaningful conclusions," write, "This will give us enough time to determine our budget." Instead of the vague "Does cross-selling have a positive impact?" use the more specific "Does cross-selling increase revenues?"

✔ **26-11.** *Break the writing into short sections.*

Once you've finished a draft of your proposal, go through it and make sure that none of your paragraphs is taller than the World Trade Center and that none of your sentences is longer than the Alaska Pipeline. If a paragraph runs more than 12 lines, think about breaking it into two or more bite-sized paragraphs. The same advice applies to sentences: If a single sentence is running more than 30 or so words, read it aloud. If you run out of breath, the sentence is too long.

Here's another way to gauge if your sentence is too long. Read it aloud to colleagues and ask them to raise their hands *at the moment they start to lose the thought of your sen-*

tence. If they raise their hands while you're still reading it, you've lost them. Solution: Break the sentence into two or more smaller sentences.

✔ 26-12. *Keep your ideas in writing parallel.*

Consistency is the key to neatness, so keep lists of bulleted items in the same format. It's easy to grasp ideas that are in parallel form—even if it's only a sentence like "Please complete the form, sign it, and send it to me." In that sentence, the lineup of verbs helps make the ideas easy to follow. When you have a list of parallel items in no particular sequence, bullet the items for easier reading. For example,

This new system:

- □ Eliminates all extra forms
- □ Increases productivity
- □ Reduces errors dramatically
- □ Eliminates extra typing

If you are asking your reader to follow you through a mathematical computation, don't put some numbers in sentences and paragraphs and display the others. Instead, break out all the computations graphically so the reader can follow you.

```
Year-to-date actuals: $834.8K
Contract amount:      $746.9K
Cost overrun TD:       $87.9K
```

John F. Kennedy's famous phrase, "Ask not what your country can do for you; ask what you can do for your country," is parallel structure at its most eloquent.

✔ 26-13. *Anticipate and defuse objections.*

Your prospective client wants to feel comfortable that you've thought of everything before making a recommendation about how you would solve his or her business problem. Therefore, you should objectively weigh the prospect's alternatives as if you were about to purchase the same services. Ask yourself: What would be the effect if I didn't purchase the service at all? Would there be negative consequences if this project didn't start for six months? What are the trade-offs in doing the project in various ways, with a wide range of possible costs?

For example, the cheapest way to do something may also be the best way—or it could be the worst way. You need to illustrate to your client at what point it makes sense to save money and when it's better to spend now and save later.

Above all, your proposal must show that you understand the client's problem and did some analysis before you started to write.

✔ **26-14.** *Avoid hedginess, subtlety, or humor.*

Avoid the urge to entertain. Better to take a sober, serious view, or else you may be perceived as frivolous. Hedging your bets by using words like *possibly, maybe, could, might, in some cases, perhaps,* or *numerous* will be viewed as wishy-washy.

Credibility is what you want to achieve, and you do that by giving concrete proof that your idea is workable. If you use hyperbole—words like *magnificent, enormous,* or *extraordinary*—you'll come across as a braggart.

✔ **26-15.** *Make a list of where key resources are located if you don't have a proposal library.*

You may not need to create a proposal library, but at least establish a file drawer that can become a repository for *all information* about clients to whom you regularly submit proposals. Include annual reports, other RFPs they've issued in the past, copies of earlier proposals you've written for them, and trade magazine and newspaper articles about them.

Also, you should have handy any biographies of people who'll participate in prospective projects as well as travel information (nearby hotels, rates, air fares). The whole purpose of this file is to prepare you to write an authoritative proposal with realistic, up-to-date data.

27

Résumés

A résumé is the equivalent of an advertisement, only the item you're promoting is yourself. Although each year dozens of books are published on résumé writing, most résumés are inadequate for the important task they undertake: presenting yourself in the most effective way possible to help you get the job you want.

One reason that résumés fail to do their job is that writing about yourself is a difficult task. Some people can't write about themselves without bragging; others cringe in embarrassment when they must highlight their accomplishments.

On the following pages, you'll see eight tips on organizing and phrasing your résumé, along with information about what you should include or omit and what is optional.

✔ **27-1.** *Make sure the look of your résumé is clean and professional.*

This may seem like obvious advice, but most of the résumés we've seen are poorly laid out and typed or reproduced with broken letters or on photocopy machines that must not have been inked properly.

Here are some general guidelines for résumé appearance. Résumés should be:

- On 8½-by-11 bond paper (16- to 24-pound weight)
- On white or off-white stock
- Typeset or typed and reproduced by photo offset; photocopies may be used if made on a superior machine; although printing produces the clearest copies, it is an expensive process that is unnecessary
- To the point, so use short sentences and short paragraphs
- Neat, so if you're updating a résumé, completely retype it; never use white-out or insert corrections on old résumés
- Easily scannable, so make sure you have plenty of white space (generally 1-inch margins on either side and ¾-inch margins on top and bottom)
- Easy on the eyes, so use underlining, boldface, italics, and bullets to vary the look of the page; choose from a variety of physical layouts, including centered and side headings that may be all uppercase or upper- and lowercase:

Company name. Office Temp

  - Designed seminar for support staff to increase productivity and develop job satisfaction

✔ **27-2.** *Use clear, specific language to describe experience.*

Some phrases sound alright until you really start to think about them. What does "personally involved in all aspects of client relations including practice development" mean to you? Any time you're involved with something, it's "personal"; what is "practice development"?

Take the phrase "provide creative services." What kind of services is the writer talking about? Beware of phrases such as "demonstrated capabilities in research, informational and copywriting" and "performed questionnaire development, computer processing of statistical data, and written interpretation of results." What is "informational" writing? And no one "performs" questionnaire development or written interpretation of results.

To avoid that kind of awkward phrasing, it's advisable to use active, or action, verbs; that is, the writer *developed* questionnaires and *interpreted* results. When explaining your accomplishments, use such verbs as *accomplished, developed, designed, managed, produced, reorganized, saved, supervised,* and *trained.*

In the "experience" section of your résumé, you should include: duties performed, responsibilities, number of people managed, achievements, and, if any of the firms you worked for are not well-known, an explanation of what each company does.

✔ **27-3.** *Keep the résumé to one or two pages.*

This is not a universally accepted rule, yet most books on résumé writing, as well as many people who receive résumés, say that short résumés are preferable to long ones, even from people with extensive experience and credentials. One frequently quoted statistic says that people scan résumés in 30 seconds—a good case for making your résumé short and succinct.

But you've done a lot in your life, you object, so how can you possibly condense all that experience into one or two brief pages? Obviously, it's not easy. Nevertheless, if you have a lot of experience you don't need to list every one of your jobs, publications, or degrees. In addition, you can condense some of the detail about any experiences that don't directly relate to the job you are seeking.

You should mention a high school or trade-school diploma only if you have no other academic credentials. If you have a college degree, list it (along with graduation date, major, and grades if they embellish your credentials) and omit mention of your high school unless you had some achievements there that are pertinent to your job plans. If you have any graduate degrees, mention those as well as your college degree.

✔ **27-4.** *Avoid lofty statements or any phrases that could be interpreted as bragging about yourself.*

For a résumé to be effective, it must separate fact from opinion. Therefore, you should avoid modifiers and opinion words and instead use concrete nouns and verbs.

What kind of words and phrases could be interpreted as bragging? Delete modifiers such as *creative, experienced, innovative,* and *accomplished.* They are all the opinions of the writer and should be left out.

Potential employers want to know what you have to offer them, not what you think about yourself.

✔ **27-5.** *List your job objective.*

Although many résumés leave out an objective, this statement, which should appear close to the top of the page, allows readers to know precisely what kind of job you're looking for. Such a statement also demonstrates just how specific and focused you are in your job search. The job objective must be written in concrete terms and with the needs of the potential employer in mind. Remember, employers want to know what they'll gain by hiring you; they aren't interested in what *you* want from them.

✔ **27-6.** *Know the elements you should omit from a résumé.*

1. *Race, religion, political affiliation.* With the strictures imposed by Equal Employment Opportunities (EEO) regulations, there is no need for you to include any personal information that might bias a potential employer against you.

2. *References.* Although you may be proud of the people who would speak highly of you, there are too many drawbacks for including either business or personal references. First, since the purpose of your résumé is to get an interview, you don't want a potential employer to call anyone before meeting you. Second, you want to make sure that your references won't be flooded with phone calls and become annoyed; instead, you want to assure them that they will only be called by select people. Third, if you are currently working, you don't want to risk having your employer find out about your job search: be assured that word gets around.

   You should always include, however, a reference statement at the bottom of the résumé that says you have references ready. A phrase such as "References available on request" works fine. By the way, avoid the antiquated "furnished upon request" phrase that has become standard issue on numerous résumés.

3. *Salary requirements.* Salary is negotiable. You don't want to be restricted by your current or past salary, so don't list it. Companies always have a salary range for a specific job, and they should let *you* know what it is before you let them know how much you want.

4. *Any negative details.* Your goal is to make your résumé as complimentary as you can without bragging. If you have an extensive work history but no high school diploma, you may want to eliminate the "education" category, for example. You should also avoid negative constructions and words such as *no, not, never,* and *delay.*

5. *Any unrelated details.* These include hobbies, extracurric-

ular activities, languages, and personal details such as finances and travel. Leave out any such detail unless it is specifically related to the job you are seeking.

6. *Abbreviations.* Choose *Street* over *St.* and *April 20, 1995* over *4/20/95.*

7. *Date or dated references.* You want to use your résumé for a while, so omit any reference to dates. Avoid statements such as "Preparing to learn…," which may become outdated before you want to update your résumé.

✔ **27-7.** *Select the appropriate format for your purpose and personality.*

The more résumé-advice books you look at, the more formats you seem to find. Each résumé expert has his or her own list of formats to follow. In addition, many books on résumé writing offer different kinds of résumés for a whole variety of job descriptions. We believe these are too confusing, so we've narrowed the choices down to three: (1) basic, (2) chronological, and (3) functional.

The *basic résumé,* which should generally be used by students or those with little job experience, follows this format:

1. Name, address, and telephone number

2. Objectives

3. Job experience or qualifications (if no job experience, or qualifications are difficult to describe, omit and place education after objectives)

4. Education (be sure to include any awards, honors, scholarships, and grade-point average if outstanding)

5. Extracurricular activities (try to stay pertinent to your job objective)

6. Foreign languages (if pertinent)

The *chronological résumé,* used by people with job experience, highlights a reversed time sequence of employment and then education. Prospective employers usually like this type of résumé because the organization makes it easy to assess qualifications.

A variation of the chronological résumé adds a summary sheet, a useful format for middle- and upper-management executives. The summary is a separate page, placed before the rest of the résumé, that condenses and interprets the qualifications of the candidate.

The *functional résumé* stresses types of work experience while playing down any particular time sequence or particular jobs. For this reason, it is sometimes used by people who want to bury certain jobs but highlight the kinds of skills they can bring to an organization. Since a résumé's primary use is to get you a job interview, it is permissible to use this format as long as you realize that you will need to explain the omissions on your résumé during an interview.

One other format worth mentioning is the *narrative* or *essay résumé,* used when you are confident of your writing skills and want your résumé to stand out from the crowd. In this format, you describe your life and work in paragraph form. Career changers may want to use this type of format, which allows them to explain their qualities and reasons for wanting change.

✔ **27-8.** *Consider adding optional information that may help strengthen your résumé.*

Such information includes:

1. Professional memberships

2. Extracurricular activities

3. Publications

4. Community involvements

5. Accreditation (CPA, honorary degrees, real estate license)

6. Reason for leaving jobs (especially if you want to emphasize career advancement)

7. Hobbies

8. Language proficiency

Remember that such information should be pertinent to your job search and somehow tie in with the rest of your résumé.

28

Presentations

In the careers of most business people, there comes a time when they must get up to deliver a presentation. That presentation may be an informal one in someone's office, or it may be in a more formal setting in front of several—sometimes hundreds of—people.

No matter what kind of presentation you're called upon to deliver, if you're like most people, you'll feel the familiar knot of fear that appears before you must speak. Giving speeches and presentations is more fearsome to most people than are natural disasters, illness—even death.

To take some of that fear away, we've come up with 40 tips to help you organize your presentation, handle graphics, take charge of the presentation environment, and field even the most difficult questions effectively.

We hope that after reading through these and applying the advice, you will face your future presentations with more confidence and pleasure.

✔ **28-1.** *Empathize with your audience's needs.*

Before you decide what you're going to say, you must identify your audience's needs and problems. Then you can begin to fashion a presentation that will be of interest to your listeners because you'll be directing your discussion to what *they* need to know, not just what *you* need to say. Even if you're presenting bad news, think about how your audience will react to that news before you start working on your presentation.

Remember that the audience wants something—to gain knowledge, to be diverted, to be informed. Identify the audience's needs by doing your homework. Once, we were asked to give a presentation about persuasive writing. Our audience was a group of sales professionals who, we found out, were great on their feet and on the telephone but hated to write selling documents. Since we only had 30 minutes for our presentation, we knew we couldn't cover the entire complex subject of persuasive writing. Instead, we focused on the benefits of writing versus speaking, and then took questions from the eager audience.

✔ **28-2.** *Think about your opening remarks from your listener's point of view.*

This is an adjunct to 28-1. The first few moments of your presentation are the most important to gain attention so your audience will want to listen to you. If you lose them in your opening, you may not get back their attention for the rest of your presentation. How do you know your listeners' points of view? First, think of yourself as part of the audience. What would motivate or inspire you? Second, compile an audience profile. What are your listeners' job functions, experience levels, attitudes toward you, attitudes to your subject? What is their main purpose in attending? What immediate and long-term use will they have from what you tell them? We'll discuss effective openings in section 28-8.

✔ **28-3.** *Think about your objective.*

Ask yourself: Why am I giving this presentation? Who is my audience, and who will do what and when? For example, if you're speaking to an alumni group to raise funds for your university, don't include details about the problems of education in America. Focus on details about the university—its diversity, its innovative approaches—and make sure you include reasons for donating to the school.

✔ **28-4.** *Identify, in the first few minutes, the reason for your presentation.*

Ask yourself if you're going to:

☐ Give information

☐ Orient or train

☐ Reach a decision

☐ Obtain a commitment

☐ Sell an idea

✔ **28-5.** *Stress benefits more than features.*

A feature is what you have to offer; a benefit is what the listener may gain from that feature. All listeners silently ask themselves as they hear you, "What's in it for me?" Even if your objective is to raise money from your audience, you must stress not only the benefits for the organization for which you are raising funds, but also the benefits to your audience of donating money (it will add to a person's prestige, self-esteem, etc.).

✔ **28-6.** *Allow time to prepare.*

Do not follow the temptation to see what miscellaneous ideas can be thrown together and go from there! Instead, use only what is most relevant to your main objective. That kind of preparation takes time—but is very worthwhile.

✔ 28-7. *Make it logical.*

The best way to think about organizing a speech is this:

- ☐ Tell 'em what you're going to tell 'em.
- ☐ Tell 'em.
- ☐ Tell 'em what you told 'em.

✔ 28-8. *Use effective openings.*

Your opening remarks are all important, so make sure they hook your audience. Use anecdotes, a rhetorical question, a provocative statement, or unusual statistics.

If you rely on your own experience for anecdotes rather than turning to reference books for them, you'll sound more sincere, you'll be sure to be original, and you'll be better able to remember details. As for asking questions, even ones that need no answer can engage your audience. If you're trying to win approval for a computerized payroll system, for example, you could begin, "If I could show you in the next few minutes how to reduce your absenteeism by 25 percent, would you consider that a worthwhile investment of your time?"

✔ 28-9. *Use your outline to write down ideas for visuals.*

Think of possible graphics to dramatize your ideas. Among your choices are illustrations, graphs, charts, tables, maps, and photos. Use visuals to illustrate ideas, but avoid mimicking the visual with your oral presentation.

✔ 28-10. *Analyze your audience's age, sex, and educational level.*

Some jokes that men find funny, women won't. Some historical references that older groups can relate to will be misunderstood by a younger crowd. Is the group sophisticated? Would they catch a reference to *West Side Story* or to *The Simpsons?* Would they relate to *Doonesbury* or to *Archie and Jughead?*

✔ **28-11.** *Make each visual stand on its own.*

Don't keep your audience hanging from visual to visual—it taxes their memory and attention span. Make each visual tell its own story without relying on other visuals to explain the words on the previous one.

✔ **28-12.** *Don't use complicated visuals.*

A complicated visual is worse than no visual at all. Ask yourself: Could my audience get this at a glance, or will people look at it and say "Huh?" A few key words or phrases per slide are all your audience can digest while still paying attention to what you're saying. And use lowercase rather than uppercase letters, which are difficult to read.

✔ **28-13.** *Understand why visuals are important.*

Although people retain only about a third of what they hear, they retain 70 percent of the information they see and hear together. Presentation charts and other visuals help shorten meeting time, focus attention, and enhance learning.

✔ **28-14.** *Achieve balanced layouts.*

Keep your visuals symmetrical; use indenting to help your reader determine which items are subgroups of larger topics.

✔ **28-15.** *Use technical data effectively.*

Keep each visual to no more than 14 lines of text. Title each visual and put simple, readable labels on graphs and tables.

✔ **28-16.** *Don't make more than three major points per visual.*

If you put too many ideas on a graphic, you begin to wear out your listener, who will probably mentally drift away from your discussion.

✔ **28-17.** *Use questions to achieve audience participation.*

Questions—by you or by your audience—help uncover any objections the audience may have to what you're saying. Probing questions can also tell you how much of what you're saying is being understood.

✔ **28-18.** *Use open questions to get a discussion going.*

If you ask questions such as "What's your opinion of report A?" instead of "Do you like report A?" you're more likely to get people to speak up and not give just one-word answers. Open questions invite a true expression of opinion or feelings and cannot be answered with a *yes* or *no*.

✔ **28-19.** *Make statistics easy to comprehend.*

Paint a picture with numbers. Instead of just saying that we use 3 million aluminum cans in one day, say, "The number of aluminum cans we use in one day could cover a football field." Round off numbers, so you'll say "almost one million customers" instead of "998,645 customers."

✔ **28-20.** *Use anecdotes.*

There's nothing like a story to grab attention (e.g., "Picture this: You're alone in the Data Center, and an outage occurs..."). Use them in any part of your presentation. In the introduction, an anecdote can personalize the subject matter; in the body of your presentation, an anecdote can elaborate on a point (e.g., "Someone used one of the on-call beepers the other day, and got me to the data center within minutes of a full-scale crisis"). In the conclusion, an anecdote can reinforce your main point and return to your opening theme.

✔ **28-21.** *Arrange audiovisual equipment well in advance.*

Before the presentation, line up the overhead, find the right focal length for easy viewing, and check that the plug is in and that the bulb is working. Make sure you know exactly where the on/off switch is so you don't have to think about it or fumble with it during your talk. Also, make sure that the plug does not present a hazard to people who may walk by.

✔ **28-22.** *Write all flipchart material on the charts in advance.*

With your flipcharts prepared ahead, you won't be under pressure to think of what to write while you're doing your presentation.

As for making effective flipcharts, here are a few tips: (1) Choose a chart that is appropriate for the design of your graphics, your height, and the size of the audience, (2) make your lettering dark enough and large enough to be read by everyone, (3) leave several blank pages between each one to allow for corrections or additions, and (4) just before you speak, remove all but one blank page before each visual so your audience won't be tempted to read a page before you want them to read it.

✔ **28-23.** *Write twice as large as you think you should!*

Always think about the person in the back of the room who may be squinting to read what you've written. People don't mind large lettering, and they don't want to squint to read tiny letters.

✔ **28-24.** *Consider your audience's economic status.*

Will you make an analogy with the stock market or the supermarket? With Bloomingdale's or Kmart? With Rolls-Royce or Toyota? Choose the images to fit the bankbook and aspirations of the people in front of you.

✔ **28-25.** *Consider how reporting relationships may affect your audience's response to your talk.*

In hierarchical organizations, if a manager is in the room with subordinates, the subordinates may not want to respond to you without first checking out the manager's response. Contrastingly, they may want to impress the manager by challenging *you.* It's best to anticipate these responses ahead of time so you can be prepared.

✔ **28-26.** *Consider your audience's likes and dislikes.*

References to an audience's preferences will make people more likely to empathize with you and consider you one of them, even if you come from another organization.

✔ **28-27.** *Avoid references to politics, religion, sex, and death.*

All these are too controversial and risky for you—unless your objective is to shock or provoke.

✔ **28-28.** *Establish your credibility.*

Early in your presentation, you need to establish your experience in your field so that people will understand why they should pay attention to what you have to say. It may be as little as a few words ("After speaking with a few dozen scientists…") or it may be a few minutes, depending on how much convincing your audience needs.

✔ **28-29.** *Keep eye contact.*

Eye contact assures your audience that you're connecting with them, and it also helps take away your self-conscious-ness and therefore defuse nervousness. Look out to see that your message is getting across. You'll be able to tell by the looks on people's faces.

With a small audience, select one person to look at and then, after you connect, move on to another person. Make a zigzag around the room, holding contact long enough to complete a brief idea or phrase.

If you have a large audience, start making eye contact with people in the back corners of the room, which are often neglected. Hold your contact from 10 to 25 seconds, and everyone in the general area will think you're looking at them.

✔ **28-30.** *Organize the colors you use.*

Remember the earth-to-sky rule—arrange colors from dark to light, bottom to top. Use the meanings of color to help convey your message: Black can indicate profit or gain;

green indicates go, readiness, growth, or money; red can indicate fear, danger, stop, error, passion, or loss; blue gives people a cool, calm, serene feeling.

Also, keep in mind that 15 percent of all men have a red/green deficiency, so make sure you mention the color of your visuals ("As you can see by the red line over here...") to make sure everyone knows what it is.

✔ **28-31.** *Use tripartite division to create a stylish ring to your phrasing.*

Presentation expert Joan Detz suggests breaking ideas into three parts. Example: "We need to develop guidelines, establish controls, and set limits." Another: "The promise is there, the logic is overwhelming, the need is great."

✔ **28-32.** *Use vertical bars, horizontal bars, and pie charts effectively.*

Use vertical bar charts for items that change over time. Use horizontal bar charts for items at a single point in time. Use pie charts to show parts of a whole—they show relative quantities by different sizes of the separate sectors and therefore are good to highlight percentages.

✔ **28-33.** *Use line, area, and text charts effectively.*

Use line charts to show trends, limiting the number of lines to no more than three or four. Use area charts to show trends over time for several variables that add up to a sum. And use text charts as a point of reference for the speaker and audience.

✔ **28-34.** *Arrive early.*

What can go wrong usually does go wrong. When you request a certain room configuration, frequently the room looks completely different when you arrive. Often, there are not enough chairs. Also, arriving early allows you to visualize yourself in the spot in which you'll be standing or sitting.

✔ **28-35.** *Smile!*

Sometimes you think you're smiling but you're really not, so make a conscious effort to look friendly.

✔ **28-36.** *Do exercises to overcome stage fright.*

Stretch and relax. One actor's technique that works wonders is to close your eyes and concentrate on one body part at a time, from the top down, and tell yourself to relax that part of your body. By the time you get down to your toes, you'll be "loose as a goose."

✔ **28-37.** *Memorize your opening and closing lines.*

You don't need to memorize any other part of your presentation, but it does help to memorize the first and last parts to give you confidence.

✔ **28-38.** *Articulate carefully.*

To practice your articulation, read aloud some of those wonderful patter songs from the operettas of Gilbert and Sullivan, or try your hand at some tongue twisters.

✔ **28-39.** *Offer to answer questions.*

When you're finished with your presentation, people may have questions. Offer to answer their questions *before* their hands shoot up. Answer each one patiently, and if a question is confusing, paraphrase it for your entire audience before attempting to answer it.

✔ **28-40.** *Take courses to refine your skills.*

It always helps to get consistent, clear, constructive feedback from an expert. If your organization offers a presentation skills course, take it. If it doesn't, call Gary Blake at (516) 767-9590 for information about The Communication Workshop's on-site seminar in presentation skills.

Index

Note: The **boldface** numbers in this index refer to tip numbers; the lightface numbers refer to page numbers.

About the Author

Gary Blake is director of The Communication Workshop, a Port Washington, New York, consulting firm that conducts business writing workshops for companies nationwide. He is the coauthor of *The Elements of Business Writing, The Elements of Technical Writing,* and *Technical Writing: Structure, Standards & Style.* For information about Dr. Blake's on-site writing seminars, please call (516-767-9590), fax (516-883-4006), or write to The Communication Workshop, 130 Shore Road, Port Washington, NY 11050.